Art of Being You

ART OF BEING YOU

Art of Being You

Breaking the Anxiety Cycle

JANNETTE MCCORMICK

Art of Being You: Breaking the Anxiety Cycle

Copyright © 2023 by Jannette McCormick

ISBN: 979-8-218-16433-1 (paperback)

Published by: Joseph's Ministry, LLC

www.josephsministryllc.com

Scripture taken from the Amplified Bible, Copyright © 2015 by The Lockman Foundation. Used by permission.

All rights reserved. Printed in the United States of America. No part of this book may be used or reproduced in any manner whatsoever without written permission from the author except in the case of brief quotations embodied in critical articles or reviews.

For my brothers. Thank you.

ART OF BEING YOU

TABLE OF CONTENTS

Aspire

Introduction 5
My Story 9

Renew

Discovery 29
The Life of a Caregiver 41
Fragments 53
Trauma or Training 63

Transform

You Are Enough 83
Joyful Beginnings 107
Boundaries 123
Believe 141
Community Building 151
Final Thoughts 169
About The Author 173
Resources 175

Aspire - Renew - Transform = The ART of being you

ART OF BEING YOU

Aspire

INTRODUCTION

"And do not be conformed to this world but be transformed and progressively changed by the renewing of your mind, so that you may prove what the will of God is, that which is good and acceptable and perfect."
– Romans 12:2

So why am I sharing my story with you? I spent a lifetime hiding my mother's "condition" to protect my family. I wanted to be the perfect "gift" of a daughter. I honestly believed taking care of my mother and being the perfect daughter was God's will for my life. I literally fell apart when I discovered that I was unintentionally wired by my parents to believe my main purpose in life was to be a caregiver for my mother. Upon my father's death, I realized (not willingly, by the way) that it was not God's will for me to exchange my life for my mother's. He did not call me to be the perfect gift to my parents. This realization left me with no idea of who I was or what my actual purpose in life entailed.

This newfound realization made me wonder, is there anyone else out there that has similar struggles? Being a young caregiver to a family member who has a mental illness is difficult and really confusing. Questions of doubt and self-worth continually invade the mind of a child caregiver. And these questions continue into adulthood. For example, what comes first? Your life or your family member's needs? Is there truly a correct answer to this question? Are you horrible for wanting a life of your own? Does your life matter? If you find yourself asking questions such as these, you are not alone.

Young caregivers, including myself, are taught to respond to life with an anxious lens. Anxiety becomes a way of life, through lessons taught by parents. Children do not necessarily inherit the anxiety disorder, although it is possible. Either way, anxiety continues within the family creating a never-ending cycle.

For readers who have not experienced caregiver responsibilities as a child or dealt with a family member struggling with mental illness, please continue reading and share this information. According to the Anxiety & Depression Association of America (ADAA), anxiety disorders are the most common mental illness in the United States. That means you most likely have a friend, co-worker, or family member that is coping with anxiety in their family.

My story is just beginning. Here's what I know at this moment.
- I was raised by a mentally ill parent.
- I was placed in a caregiver role as a child due to necessity – that is not normal or healthy.

- My parents loved me and did the best they could under the circumstances.
- I am not defined by my mother's illness.
- I am not perfect, nor will I (or anyone) ever be perfect. And that's okay.
- Secrets do not protect families, they damage individuals.
- God has given me gifts to help others (not just my family).

You may notice that each chapter begins with a scripture from the Bible. I am a Christian, and I strive to live my life according to the principles outlined in the Bible. Biblical scriptures are designed to educate and provide hope to the reader. Hope should be at the center of our heart and should drive our actions. The scriptures cited are but a few that guided me through my journey of discovering my purpose.

My intent is not to place blame, but to discover what negative impacts exist due to the mental illness suffered by my family and find ways to minimize these consequences for the future. In other words, I want a healthy, joyful life for myself, my husband and my children.

What's next? The following pages outline my personal story, research I found helpful, and guidance provided to me through studying scriptures. If you have similar experiences, I want you to know that you are not alone. My hope is this information will shed light on the effect being a child caregiver has on adults and provide a resource to help break the anxiety cycle.

MY STORY

"And you will know the truth and the truth will set you free."
– John 8:32

In 2019, my father was diagnosed with an aggressive cancer that had no cure. My father's last direction to me was, "Take care of your mother." For this reason, my brothers and I met to discuss how we would carry out his wish. We all had careers and families of our own. My children were still in school and the youngest of the bunch. My mother's needs had not changed; she could not be left alone for any amount of time. She claimed she would have a panic attack that would kill her. We had never tested it.

As usual, I developed a few scenarios for my mother's care to share with my brothers. I knew this conversation would be my only chance at getting their help in activating whichever plan seemed most appropriate. I also knew I could not do this alone and hoped my brothers would help.

To be honest, I was not as prepared as I normally am in these types of situations. My whole life was about taking charge in situations my mother could not handle. This was just another situation to manage. But I found myself not being able to "think through" options. I would physically and mentally "freeze" when trying to take any sort of action concerning the care of my mother. It was aggravating and scary.

The conversation with my brothers did not go as I had planned. My brothers started the conversation by telling me it was not my responsibility to make my mother's decisions. My sisters-in-law told me it was not fair that my parents put me in a caregiver role as a child, and that it was not healthy. All agreed it was time for my mother to own up to the decisions my parents had made earlier in their lifetime and care for herself. That meant she would have to learn to live alone or be placed in a nursing home. The decision was hers to make, not mine. It was like a load of bricks had just toppled on top of me. I couldn't breathe. All I could squeak out was, "How do I say no?" My brothers were quick to answer. "You can't, but we can."

My brothers recognized my parents had spent a lifetime "wiring" me to believe it was my responsibility to care for my mother. She came first, my life was secondary. When I became an adult with my own family, my parents helped me tremendously. But when a crisis arose, I was sucked back into the caregiver role established in my youth. My brothers saw it but felt powerless to help. My brothers viewed my father's death as an opening to help me break away. They were right. Even so, I felt like a failure.

My life was built on being successful. I was considered one of the smartest kids in my class. I was class president. I was voted most likely to succeed. I was the first in my family to graduate college. I received promotion after promotion at work celebrating my efforts. In my mind, all of this was due to the gifts given to me by God. Imagine my horror when I realized my gifts were the result of my parents conditioning me. I never had a childhood. My childhood was nowhere near normal. I was not special. I was a resource.

As you can imagine, a mini emotional breakdown followed. My brothers did take control of my mother's care. She did make a tough decision, and with my brothers' help, she learned how to stay by herself. This was a freeing moment for my mother that we all celebrated. However, inside, I was so mad. Now, when she has no options, she can care for herself? Why didn't she care enough for me to do that before? Why did I have to miss out on so many opportunities as a child? My brothers and I had to suffer through a childhood filled with anxiety and no way to control it. It was not fair.

I felt weak. I was weak enough to be programmed to think it was my responsibility to care for my mother. I was too weak to recognize this unhealthy perception as an adult. I was too weak to even know which of my thoughts and actions were healthy and which were fueled by the anxiety wired into me during childhood. I feared that I had inadvertently "wired" my sons for the same damaged view of life. I realized most, if not all, of the challenges my marriage faced were my fault – programming error. I was not the solution; I was the problem. How did I not see this?!

This led me to do what any rational person would, I searched the internet for articles, books, podcasts, anything that described the effects of being raised by an anxious parent. Not a lot surfaced. What did appear were articles on mental illness, trauma and how to avoid raising anxious children. Another breakdown followed.

The second hardest reality for me to accept was that I was a victim. The few articles I found on being raised by an anxious, mentally ill parent all stated that being raised in this type of environment traumatized the child. According to these articles, adults raised by a mentally ill parent needed to seek professional help to process the trauma and discover healthy ways to relate to others. Trauma. Victim. I was not in control. I was my mother. Professional counseling followed.

Back Story

In order to move forward, you need to understand where you have been. The first step in overcoming the anxiety cycle for me was to revisit my youth and view it without the caregiver lens. The purpose is not to place blame for what occurred in the past. The purpose is to understand the situations that led me to where I am today.

I am the youngest of three children and the only girl. Most would think that family placement would also make me spoiled and wanting for nothing. Unfortunately, in my family, it made me the one that drew the shortest straw.

One of my favorite childhood pictures is of me when I was roughly four years old. I had a football uniform on, helmet and all, and I was holding my new baby doll. It was Christmas time. All the gifts had been opened, but the thrill of the new toys was still in the air. My parents bought football uniforms for my brothers to wear for fun during family scrimmages. My mother didn't want me to feel left out, so my parents purchased a uniform for me as well. Don't be mistaken, I had no desire to play football in the yard with my brothers. That would have been a death wish, but the uniform was really "pretty." It had white pants, a bright red shirt and a helmet to protect me from the surprise "nougee" attacks my brothers planned for me on a regular basis. Two against one – totally not fair, but that's a story for another time.

When I wore the uniform, I felt connected to my brothers which was a rare but wonderful feeling. When I look at the picture now, it seems somewhat ironic. A portrait of a young child illustrating that she is capable of being many things: a mom to a doll, a football player, an annoying sister or whatever is needed at the given time.

I was raised by parents that loved me and tried to be supportive in their own way. So much so, that I convinced myself that I had the most "normal" childhood of all my friends. My parents were not divorced. My parents were not alcoholics. My parents did not have affairs with married individuals. My parents did not hit me. In the 1970's and 1980's, avoiding these types of situations was quite a feat. However, my family had a secret that my brothers and I protected for the sake of our parents and ourselves.

I grew up in small town USA. There were churches on every street corner and generations of families knew each other. Connections developed through attending school together, going to the same church or simply being related to one another. In junior high school, I had an ongoing argument with a classmate as to whether he was my cousin or not. He insisted we were "third" cousins, of which I disagreed. Turns out he was right!

My parents met at church in this small town. My father was one of twelve children. The girls in town were ecstatic when his family moved to town – more boys for the picking! Most of my aunts and uncles all went to school together, and they had unlimited stories to share with us of days gone past. The one guiding principle both my parents' families instilled in their children was Christian faith.

My parents married shortly after graduating high school. My father worked as a concrete finisher, and my mother had employment at a local ministry as clerical support. My father did not want a family, but my mother always felt she was destined to be a mom. It was a surprise when she became pregnant within their first year of marriage.

My father did not have an easy childhood. His father was ill for most of my father's life, and the family was on welfare benefits for several years due to this. He was born in the last "third" of twelve children. His father passed away when he was a teenager. My father struggled with the loss, and his faith began to slip away because of bitterness and anger. Due to his childhood experiences, my father did not want a family. It just happened.

My mother's childhood, in comparison, was easier. Her father worked in the cotton gins and managed livestock for ranchers. Her mother worked, as needed, to keep the family afloat. My mother had two brothers and one sister. She was the middle child, being the third child born. Her family had what was needed, not much more. Grandpa was nervous by nature which was a trait passed down by his mother. It did not prevent him from functioning in society, but it was more of an annoyance to my grandma. Grandma was strong-willed and seemed to be able to manage just about anything. My mother took after her father.

My mother was considered by family members to be a "nervous" person. To my friends, she was a strict parent. In reality, she had a mental illness that, at the time, medical professionals did not understand. My mother would have a severe panic attack if left alone for any amount of time. She could not go into public areas – this included stores, office buildings, large gatherings of any sort, church and school functions. Her "nervousness" was debilitating.

I spent my early years traveling with my mother to relatives' houses, usually one of my grandmothers' homes, to stay until my father came home from work. He was self-employed and worked long hours. Then, when my brothers and I were old enough (in my mother's mind), we stayed home with our mother.

My mother did not always suffer from this level of anxiety. It developed when she experienced a traumatic event. My mother almost died while giving birth for the first time. In the 1960's, family members, including the father, were not allowed in the birthing rooms. My mother was in a room with other women working through contractions and waiting for the doctor to say, "It's time!" I can only imagine how frightening that must have been for her.

My brother was breached, and for reasons I do not know, a c-section was not performed. My mother lost a large amount of blood. Fortunately, my father and his brother were the same blood type as my mother. Each had to provide several pints of blood to keep my mother alive. It may seem odd to some people that my mother's brother-in-law stepped in to help. In my family, that's just what you did. Family always supported each other.

My mother was not able to handle the anxiety and fear that followed this event. It morphed her from being a "nervous" person to having an anxiety disorder that prevented her from managing her own life. At that time, medical professionals did not view anxiety as a mental health disorder. In fact, mental illness was not discussed at all. You were either crazy or not. That simple. My mother was referred to psychiatrists who prescribed Valium and told her she needed to "work through" her fears. She was told by professionals that it was all in her head. My mother gave up and my extended family took care of her until I was old enough to take their place.

Why Me?

When I was very young, my mother found a book of baby names and showed me the "meaning" of my name – God's gift. I still remember her showing me the book. My parents viewed my "gift" as being there to help.

I was raised that God gives each person a purpose in life. Our goal as Christians is to follow that purpose in all we do. In my mind, being God's gift meant I was to care for my parents. That meant support my father by helping with things that my mother couldn't do. It also meant staying with my mother so she wouldn't have a panic attack.

As an adult, blessed with two children of my own, I know now that I was not a "gift" but a resource. My parents were in a desperate situation and made decisions that were not in the best interest of me or my brothers. I'm not sure I would have done much better, given the circumstances.

My father was under a lot of stress trying to earn a living for the family and find care for my mother. Most days he came home angry and tired not wanting to have much to do with us. I was usually sent in to test his "temperament" because he was the easiest on me. My father did not physically harm anyone, but his words could slash right through your heart. It was like walking on a tightrope. One moment you're balanced, and everyone is cheering you; and, in the next moment, you lose your footing and pray there is a net to catch your fall. You never knew if Dad would curse at you or joke with you.

My mother was no help. If it was a difficult night, she would go to her room and cry. Nerves. If it was a good night, she would act as if we were the happiest family on earth. In either circumstance, we did not talk about it. We were expected to manage it.

Our father was focused on working to keep the family afloat. There were brief periods of silliness in which we felt like a normal family, and these periods were cherished by all – at least from my viewpoint. More often, there were periods of being ignored, literally. If my father was overwhelmed with work, home, family, he would completely ignore everyone in the family. It didn't matter if you were the reason for his frustration. It didn't matter if he promised to do something with you the night before. He ignored you.

There were times I would stand in front of my father, who was sitting in his recliner as he did every night, and ask him a question. He wouldn't even look at me. He went about his evening as if we didn't exist. If I was brave, I would push his arm repeatedly saying, "Daddy, Daddy, Daddy." Nothing. Now I understand that my father was probably experiencing depression. As a child, I just thought he didn't care. So did my brothers.

Me and Mom

My mother was an anxious person even before her traumatic experience, but that experience seemed to magnify her anxiety. My mother viewed everything as having a potential negative impact to our lives. She had to be able to "see" us if we were outside of the house. I was only allowed to ride my bike in the street adjacent to our house that was viewable through the windows. Seriously. Luckily, our house sat on a corner lot, so I had two streets I could travel. My mother believed if I was out of sight, something bad would happen to me. At the time, I just thought my mother was overprotective.

My mother did not talk to me about "girl" things. She taught me household responsibilities that assisted her needs. I know how to cook basic meals, do laundry, clean a house properly, and pay bills thanks to my mother. I watched my friends go shopping at the mall and have lunch dates with their moms. They talked about boys, clothing and makeup (lots of makeup – it was the 80's!).

The closest bonding time I had with my mom was watching soap operas. I learned how relationships with the opposite sex worked by watching General Hospital and All My Children. You see where I'm going with this don't you? Young love was always disrupted by betrayal and lies. Forgiveness would be granted, but it would be followed by more betrayal by someone that would tear couples and families apart. So, I expected my first love to be grand – something like the scene from *Sixteen Candles* when the gorgeous guy shows up at the girl's house on her birthday to whisk her away to share a beautiful birthday cake with him in honor of her presence on earth. My expectations were a little high.

On the flip side, I also expected and anticipated that my boyfriends would lie to me. I was always on the defensive, waiting for the betrayal to happen. I developed this fear early in life. In fact, when I was six, I was convinced my father was cheating on my mother with an ex-girlfriend from high school. Six. I was terrified he would leave. I never talked to my mother about this fear. We didn't talk about those types of things. Instead, we watched One Life to Live.

What I didn't realize was that my mother's anxiety was being hard wired into my way of thinking. As a parent, I would become anxious whenever I had to leave the boys anywhere.

Taking them to daycare so I could work was almost unbearable. Other moms would visit on their lunch hour just to ease their concerns. I couldn't do that. If I visited, I would have to experience the anxiety I felt twice in one day. That was unbearable. I was also convinced it would be bad for the boys. I assumed that they felt the same separation anxiety that I did. Whether that was true or not, my actions were keeping the anxiety train moving in our family. It had to stop.

I wish I could report that I realized these behaviors were unhealthy and stopped them shortly after my sons started going to daycare. I didn't. The boys were driving themselves to school by the time I realized I was allowing my mother's fears to affect how I raised the boys. The same fears that plagued my mother were passed down to me through behaviors I learned watching her. I continued the madness, trying to protect my sons from literally everything (perceived and real).

Fortunate for me, my husband recognized my actions were based on learned fears and challenged me every step of the way. His strength offset the negative impact my fears could have had on our sons. Although I spent many nights frustrated and mad at my husband during that time, I now am so grateful that he watched over our sons and protected them from my anxiety.

College Bound!

Throughout my life, when making a decision, I factored in whether or not this decision would affect my mother's life. If yes, I didn't consider it. The one exception was my decision to attend college. I decided in third grade that I wanted to attend college after high school. No one in my immediate family, and very few in my extended family (aunts, uncles, cousins), went to college. When I was in third grade, my aunt stopped by to visit. She had a course book from a college class she was taking at the time. It took her several years, but she eventually got her degree. She let me thumb through the pages while she talked about everything she was learning. I was hooked. I was college bound from that moment on.

During my junior year in high school, work for my father was difficult to find due to the economic situation in our state. Dad traveled to other states for work. He would come home most weekends. At the time, it was just me and my mother at home. My brothers had moved out after high school. My grandmother helped, but I was ultimately responsible for staying with my mother – except while I was in school. On the weekends Dad returned home, I would escape with friends and pretend I had a normal teenaged life.

During my senior year in high school, my dad was offered work in California. My dream had always been to attend college in California. Beaches, surfboards and boardwalks called my name. To be clear, I only wanted a surfboard for decoration – I can't even swim! Again, due to Dad working out of state, it was just me and Mom at the house during my final year of high school. Unfortunately, Dad couldn't come home as much, but he made it back for my senior activities. I honestly don't remember much that happened these two years. I do remember feeling trapped.

Once I graduated from high school, my parents and brothers all moved to California. My parents wanted me to move with them and attend college in California. That had been my dream – *right*? That's when I realized the dream wasn't about California specifically (although I still want a surfboard), it was about escaping my responsibilities at home. I wanted a break. My grandparents offered their house as my "home base," so I could stay in Oklahoma and attend college. The guilt was overwhelming, but the four years that followed were some of the happiest years of my life.

Reality Bites

I'm not sure what is more difficult to face, the past or the future. My rose-colored glasses were shattered when my father passed away. The reality of my youth became clear, and I had to face the everlasting effects of being raised in a difficult family situation. Feelings that I never allowed myself to experience came rushing to the surface sporadically. I had no control of my emotions. I knew I needed to allow myself to feel the despair, fear, anger and frustration that had been bottled inside me, but that allowance didn't fit into my neatly planned life.

Unfortunately, that didn't seem to matter to my emotions. They were determined to be recognized and felt. There was no rhyme or reason to when the emotions surfaced. I remember sitting in my living room watching a funny movie when an overwhelming sense of sadness came over me. I started crying, quietly at first, but full-on sobs soon developed.

Another time, I was at work in my office, and I started crying uncontrollably. I had been reading emails. That's it. There was nothing that happened that warranted a breakdown, but there I was crying away, feeling overwhelmed and having no idea about how to control my emotions. I didn't even know why I was feeling this way!

Emotions we do not allow ourselves to feel do not magically go away. The body stores them in what I'll call the holding cell. Once the cell is full, the doors burst open, and it's a party. Because of my mother's mental illness, I had to keep a calm environment. I learned at an early age to keep my feelings bottled until I was alone and could deal quietly with them.

My holding cell was more like a holding facility, with many rooms – which I needed – because withholding my emotions didn't end when I moved away from home and started my own family. It continued. The final explosion that brought my holding facility down was the combination of my father passing away, the responsibility I felt for my mother, and my brothers offering help to me. BOOM! The emotions party was in full swing at this point. I had no idea how to control it, but I needed to figure it out quickly. I knew if I didn't face it, my anxiety would grow out of control – just like my mother's anxiety. I couldn't do that to my family. I had to accept help.

Challenging times lead to stronger faith if we endure. In James, the author writes,

> Consider it nothing but joy, my brothers and sisters, whenever you fall into various trials. Be assured that the testing of your faith produces endurance. And let endurance have its perfect result and do a thorough work, so that you may be perfect and completely developed, lacking in nothing. If any of you lacks wisdom, he is to ask God, who gives to everyone generously and without rebuke or blame, and it will be given to him (James 1:2-5).

I knew that to face the reality of my past, I would need wisdom. So, I began to ask God for wisdom not only in my everyday life but in overcoming any negative impacts of my childhood that needed to be addressed. It wasn't just my life that was being affected. My sons' futures depended on me breaking the anxiety cycle and creating a healthy environment for our family.

ART OF BEING YOU

Renew

DISCOVERY

"The night is almost gone and the day is almost here. So let us fling away the works of darkness and put on the armor of light."
– Romans 13:12

My world was turned upside down. I had to make sense of it, and that meant researching everything. I read anything I could find on anxiety. I researched the effect being raised by a mentally ill parent had on children. I needed to understand why God would allow me to be in a caregiver role if it was not healthy for me.

Before the death of my father, I never allowed myself to question why I was given this responsibility. That somehow felt like I was being disrespectful to my parents. Unknowingly, I buried those feelings to protect my parents and myself. I realize now that keeping unresolved feelings bottled up for years does not protect but creates additional problems. I needed to understand the why and what of my childhood experience in order to renew myself and move forward with my life.

Growing up, I did not view my mother as having a mental illness. In my mind, mental illness referred to bipolar disorder, schizophrenia and similar conditions. A basic Google search for mental illness pulls a wealth of information on a variety of mental illnesses in today's society. However, anxiety disorders generally only receive an honorable mention. Why is this?

According to the Anxiety & Depression Association of America, anxiety disorders are the most common mental illness in the United States with 40 million adults (age 18 and older) affected every year. Although anxiety disorders are highly treatable, slightly less than 37% of people affected with anxiety receive treatment. The most common reason cited for not seeking treatment is cost.

What is an anxiety disorder? As defined by the Mayo Clinic:

> Experiencing occasional anxiety is a normal part of life. However, people with anxiety disorders frequently have intense, excessive and persistent worry and fear about everyday situations. Often, anxiety disorders involve repeated episodes of sudden feelings of intense anxiety and fear or terror that reach a peak within minutes (panic attacks). These feelings of anxiety and panic interfere with daily activities, are difficult to control, are out of proportion to the actual danger and can last a long time. You may avoid places or situations to prevent these feelings.

Risk factors for having an anxiety disorder includes genetics, brain chemistry, personality and life events. Depression and anxiety often go hand in hand with treatment needed for both illnesses. In addition, many individuals who have an anxiety disorder may have another disorder or physical illness as well. For example, posttraumatic stress disorder (PTSD) and obsessive-compulsive disorder (OCD) are closely related to anxiety disorders. In reality, a person can be suffering from an anxiety disorder, depression and PTSD all at once. I believe that was the case for my mother.

Discovering that there are several types of anxiety disorders and reading through the explanations of each helped me realize that my mother's issues were truly a medical condition warranting treatment. In the 1970's, anxiety was viewed as a "nervous" personality trait that one could overcome on their own if desired. This, of course, couldn't be farther from the truth.

Today, anxiety is recognized as a mental illness that can be treated, but the perception of anxiety has not changed much. As stated earlier, around 37% suffering from an anxiety disorder in the United States receive treatment. And that is from a pool of individuals that have been diagnosed by a medical professional. What about the families that are hiding their loved one's illness due to the stigma mental illness has in communities? How many people are suffering not realizing that advances have been made in mental health treatment that could help them live a healthier, more balanced life?

Listed below are the more common types of anxiety disorders with a brief description as defined by the U.S. Department of Health and Human Services and the National Institute of Mental Health. Remember, it is not uncommon for a person to experience more than one disorder at the same time.

Generalized Anxiety Disorder (GAD) – characterized by chronic anxiety, exaggerated worry and tension, even when there is little to nothing to provoke it. Major depression often accompanies GAD.

Panic Disorder (PD) – unexpected and repeated episodes of intense fear accompanied by physical symptoms including chest pain, heart palpitations, shortness of breath, dizziness or abdominal distress.

Social Anxiety Disorder (SAD) – overwhelming anxiety and excessive self-consciousness in everyday social situations. SAD can be related to specific events such as public speaking or so broad that symptoms arise anytime an individual is around other people.

Specific Phobias – intense and irrational fear of something that possess little to no danger. OCD and PTSD (see descriptions below) are related to phobias. Individuals may experience these disorders along with specific phobias and depression.

Stress – (surprised?) How you respond to stress may result in anxiety.

Obsessive-Compulsive Disorder (OCD) – reoccurring thoughts sometimes accompanied by repetitive behaviors such as handwashing, counting, or cleaning performed in an attempt to stop the thoughts. The repetitive behaviors temporarily provide relief from anxious thoughts.

Post-traumatic Stress Disorder (PTSD) – anxiety develops after exposure to a terrifying event where physical harm occurred or was threatened.

Major Depressive Disorder – This is the leading cause of disability in the United States for ages 15 to 44 (ADAA). This disorder causes severe symptoms that affect how a person, feels, thinks and handles everyday life. Symptoms must be present for at least two weeks and include (but not limited to) sadness, anxiety, hopelessness, irritability, worthlessness, helplessness, loss of interest and decreased energy.

Persistent depressive disorder (PDD) – formerly referred to as dysthymia, this is a major depressive disorder that lasts for two or more years. Individuals may experience episodes of major depression with periods of less severe symptoms.

Educating myself on the different types of anxiety disorders brought clarity to my situation. I wasn't making a big deal out of nothing. My mom has a medical condition that is shared by many people across the globe. My parents did their best to manage her condition and provide a safe environment for the family.

It is important to remember that a child learns behaviors through example. For young caregivers, our adult example includes behaviors intertwined with anxiety. So, we are taught to respond to life with an anxious lens. Anxiety becomes a way of life, through lessons taught by parents and not necessarily due to inheriting the anxiety disorder. It can also be a mixture of both.

Two areas that are common for child caregivers to struggle with during (and after) childhood include separation anxiety and social anxiety.

Separation Struggles

I had a tough time transitioning to kindergarten. My mother told the teacher it was probably due to the recent loss of my great-grandfather. Grandpa Jim was my mother's grandfather. He lived in a retirement apartment just a few blocks from where we lived. I would occasionally visit him with my grandma and mom. Due to medical issues, I did not understand, he was only able to eat baby food and sardines. At least that's all I ever saw him eat. We'd have several jars of both for him. Crazy combination but it seemed perfectly logical to me at the time. He always had a smile for me, and I enjoyed visiting him. Grandpa Jim was the first relative I was close to that died. It made perfect sense that this would affect me, and I would have separation anxiety. However, looking back I do not believe that was my issue.

Many young caregivers have separation anxiety due to their responsibilities of caring for a parent. The thought that a parent may need something, and they are not there to help is frightening. As a child, I had the occasional nightmares involving Big Foot or vampires. However, most of my nightmares involved me being away from home and suddenly realizing that I was supposed to be at home with my mom. The fear that something bad happened to my mom because I wasn't there was horrific – even worse than meeting Big Foot.

To this day, I vividly remember one such dream. In my dream, I really wanted to go trick or treating with my friends. My mother told me I wouldn't have time between school and when I was supposed to be home with her. I went anyway, thinking I could squeeze in a few houses and still be home in time. I was having so much fun I forgot about Mom. My aunt pulls up in a car and tells me my mom is in danger, and it is my fault. She kept asking me why I didn't go home like I was told to do. That's where the dream ended. I woke up without knowing if my mom was okay.

This type of fear stays with you as a child. Every day the fear that I would be late from school or forget to do something that my mom needed created a level of anxiety that I had to manage. The separation anxiety I experienced in kindergarten had nothing to do with losing Grandpa Jim. It was caused by my fear of being away from home and not being able to provide my mother the care she might need.

As an adult, this fear has morphed into a fear of being late. My anxiety level rises anytime I think I am going to be late (or even exactly on time) to an event. To avoid this feeling, I always arrive several minutes early to meetings, appointments, events or even family get-togethers. The fear I developed as a child continues to manifest in my adult life.

Social Struggles

Young caregivers also struggle with social anxiety. When a parent has a mental illness, the focus is on their care. Many times, parents forget children need to learn how to interact socially. Growing up, I did not have "play dates" with friends. The only other children I interacted with were my cousins. I only saw them on special occasions and holidays. I entered kindergarten with extraordinarily little experience in making friends, playing with other children, and being outside my home.

When my older brother started to learn how to read, I was right by his side. I was born with a love for books. I so desperately wanted to be able to read a book by myself. So, it was a shock to my mother when I was placed in the lowest level reading group in kindergarten. The teacher told my mother that I was slow and could not read at the same level as others.

My teacher would have everyone sit in a circle and take turns reading out loud in front of each other. Based on how well you read your passage, she would then separate everyone into smaller groups. When it was my turn, I wouldn't read. My teacher assumed it was because I didn't have the ability to read. In actuality, I was terrified to read in front of other students. What if I messed up? Would they laugh at me? My mother convinced the teacher to allow me to read to her privately. By myself, I was able to read the most difficult passage to my teacher.

My mother told my teacher I was extremely shy. In reality, this was one way my social anxiety manifested itself. I still struggle with social anxiety, just in different ways. I no longer have a fear of public speaking, but I do struggle with maintaining close relationships. The same questions of inadequacy and what if I embarrass myself run through my mind.

To this day, the thought of having to attend a networking session for work sends chills down my spine. It's not a concern of how to connect with a person. I enjoy meeting new people and learning about their experiences. I also have no problem sharing professional experiences with others. What I fear is when the conversation turns to me, and it's my turn to share personal experiences.

It's in that moment when you must be vulnerable to be authentic that my mind races with thoughts of inadequacy. What if they ask details about my childhood? I can't reveal my family's secret. What if they realize I'm not perfect? Ridicule is sure to follow. What if they realize I don't belong or deserve to be here? Alarms go off in my head and my defense mechanisms come to life! I subconsciously put up a barrier preventing me from developing close relationships on both a professional and personal level.

Level Up!

It is so easy to fall into the trap of measuring our value by the world's standards. Worldly success is often measured by the title you have at work, the amount of money you make, or even how popular you are on social media. None of that matters to God. Our value comes from Him. It cannot be earned. Remember, God has placed you here for His purpose, and your value comes from Him. It does not come from your past, from the world, or from any one person. Your value comes from God alone.

There is so much general information out there on anxiety. The challenge is to piece together portions of information that address your situation. As a child, I struggled with social and separation anxiety. As an adult, that struggle evolved into a fear of rejection, among other things. Your struggles may be different, and that is okay. The key is to own your past, your story, and discover how it has impacted your life.

You may be thinking, "I lived it, what else do I need to do to own it?!" You need to understand the *why* behind the actions that were taken in the past. For me, that meant I needed to understand the medical condition my mother battled. I needed to look at our family situation from everyone's perspective (my mother's, my brothers', my father's, and my own).

I also had to allow myself to be angry, sad, frustrated and scared about my childhood, without feeling guilty. When my father died, I not only lost him, but I lost my childhood. I had created this perception of my childhood that was not real. I only remembered the positive things and minimized any negative situations – if I remembered them at all. This is not healthy.

It's time to "level up"! Embrace all aspects of your childhood experience: the good, the bad and the ugly. Celebrate the positive impact it has made on your life. Rewire the negative behaviors you learned. When we accept all of who we are, we become a stronger version of ourselves. Anxiety is a part of my life and will always be there, but it does not define me.

THE LIFE OF A CAREGIVER

"The light shines in the darkness, and the darkness has not overcome it".
– John 1:5

Part of my personal discovery process involved searching for others with experiences like mine. I came across a study completed in 2016 by Lynne McCormack, PhD, Sarah White, DClinPsych and Jose Cuenca, PhD, entitled "A Fractured Journey of Growth: Making Meaning of a *'Broken'* Childhood and Parental Mental Ill-health." The study was unique because the research was based on the experiences of the child caregiver not the mentally ill parent.

What is a child caregiver exactly? Child caregivers are under the age of 18 who regularly provide care, assistance, or support to another family member. These caregivers assume responsibility well above the level associated with their age and most often at the adult level. The family member being cared for often has a chronic illness, mental health problem or other condition that requires care, support or supervision. The child caregiver role also includes children who care for parents that have a substance abuse problem.

As I read through the pages of the study, I realized my childhood was very much like the seven participants interviewed. The make-up of my family and the families who participated in the study all differed; some participants had both parents living in the household, and some only one parent. Some had siblings, and others did not. Regardless of the situation, the struggles faced by the child caregivers were the same.

Have you ever felt isolated? How about betrayed? This is not uncommon for young caregivers. The study revealed that children who grow up with a parent affected by mental illness often experience distress, stigma, shame, social isolation and betrayal. Many of these emotions stem from childhood needs not being met. My mother was restricted by her illness. I was fortunate that my father stayed and did his best to take care of the family, but there was only so much he could handle.

In our household, my mother's needs came first and then everyone else's needs were considered. This is common in families with mental health illness. Unfortunately, this lends to children feeling betrayed by their own parents. A feeling of insignificance and low self-esteem often follow. However, when placed in a caregiver role, the child is given a purpose. This helped me develop adaptive skills such as resilience and problem-solving. As an adult, these skills have helped me to be successful. As a child, they helped me survive in an unstable environment.

There's a paragraph from the study I want to share with you. It really hit home for me.

> These participants described an existence of isolation and abandonment in childhood, where their personal and emotional safety was secondary to others' needs. This extended to feeling invisible where not only parents, but society seemed unaware of their plight and social disconnectedness. They spoke of not feeling secure or valued, with unpredictable parenting. A sense of being betrayed compounded feelings of guilt and sadness. Behaviors learned to hide the truth of family life led to secrecy and shame. Safety and survival absorbed their energy as they navigated their way through reversed-parenting their unwell parent and the 'never-ending madness'. However, these experiences were described as being a double-edged sword. They recognized as adults inner strengths of empathy and compassion and their ability to resource themselves in difficult situations had emerged from their childhood plight. They recognized education as a conduit out of their childhood despair and made conscious decisions about their own way of being in a world without mental illness.

These are my people. When I read this passage, for the first time in my life, I didn't feel alone. It was like the researchers reached into my head and pulled these words out. I realized, that as an adult I had buried these feelings deep inside of me instead of working through them. Now, decades later, the feelings resurfaced and here I am reliving the struggles of my youth.

Study Take-aways

The study identified six "themes" youth experienced when brought up in an unpredictable environment due to a parent struggling with mental illness.

1. Who Cares – Nobody Cares
2. Trauma and Betrayal
3. Transferring Distress
4. Duck Weaving and Staying Safe
5. Growing Myself Up
6. Transforming a Broken Childhood

Let's take a closer look at each theme.

<u>Who Cares – Nobody Cares</u>

Child caregivers often feel alone, vulnerable and helpless. As mentioned before, the mentally ill parent's needs come first and often overshadow the needs of other family members. This lends to the child feeling unimportant. In addition, society seems to turn a blind eye on a young caregiver's plight. In the child's eyes, other families are normal – not their own. I felt this way. My family was different, therefore it had to be broken. I felt ashamed and wanted to hide our "brokenness" from the outside world. I wanted to be normal.

What I didn't understand at the time, was by not talking about my struggles, society was not given the opportunity to help me. By sharing, I could have connected with others sharing the same challenges and possibly helped them, as well as myself. In essence, I isolated myself because of fear associated with the stigma of mental illness – the fear of rejection.

As a child caregiver, especially one who has been socially isolated due to a parent's illness, the thought of reaching out for help never occurs. Our role is to provide the help to the ones we love, not seek it; since no one offers help to us, it feels very much like no one cares.

Trauma and Betrayal

Child caregivers have to overcome struggles on a daily basis. Most children have their parents available to guide them through the challenges associated with youth. Children with a mentally ill parent often find themselves navigating alone while helping their parents with everyday care issues. Unfortunately, mentally ill parents are overwhelmed by their own needs and often fail to provide a safe and nurturing environment for their children. This leaves the child feeling betrayed and unworthy of love. Child caregivers can be traumatized by the reoccurring struggles they face in the unstable home environment. You always feel "on guard" waiting for the next problem to arise.

This is the part of my childhood I chose not to remember as an adult. As I read the challenges faced by the study participants, memories of my childhood came rushing back. For me, it was not physical harm that I feared, it was emotional. Not knowing if my mom would be having a "good" day, or whether my father would be happy or mad when I got home kept me on edge. How I responded to my family depended on the environment at home which was ever-changing. This heightened sense of being on guard affects not only a child's emotional well-being, but the added stress can affect their physical health.

Ducking, Weaving and Staying Safe

Children raised in an unstable environment learn early in life how to keep themselves and usually other family members safe. For me, it was keeping my mother calm and my father happy. If I accomplished this, our home environment remained stable. I learned to "read" the room and adjust my behavior to help promote the desired environment. Staying out of the way, changing behaviors, and helping others were all techniques I used to create an environment I perceived to be safe.

This skill was valued by my family members. I was often praised for my "maturity." Oddly, as an adult, I am also rewarded at work for exhibiting the same behavior. Fitting in became a survival skill. Unfortunately, that means you have to always be on alert, assessing your environment. You can never relax and just be yourself.

Transferring the Distress

Not knowing the complete story behind a parent's illness leaves room for a child's imagination to go wild. Confusion leads to children blaming themselves for their parent's illness. The secrecy around the illness creates confusion for children and leads them to be ashamed, anxious and stressed. Imagine trying to make sense of all these negative emotions with no parent to guide you. In essence, children believe they are responsible for their parent's illness.

This theme is hard to explain unless you have experienced caring for a mentally ill parent. As a child, I thought my actions and behaviors directly affected the severity of my mother's illness. I took responsibility for her good days and her bad days. In addition, trying to understand a parent is ill even though there are no physical signs of sickness is hard for a child. In my case, even my parents didn't have a true understanding of my mother's condition. How could they explain it to me and my brothers? Understanding what caused my mother's anxiety would have helped me not transfer the distress or feel responsible for my mother's condition. We will explore the need to understand this in more detail within the "Fragments" chapter.

Growing Myself Up

As stated before, the focus of the family is caring for the mentally ill parent. Many times, the needs of the children are secondary. Child caregivers have to navigate "growing up" with little assistance.

Participants of the study had positive and negative effects due to their childhood experiences. Positive effects included being able to easily show empathy and compassion to others, exhibiting resiliency even in difficult situations, and having a strong, moral character. As an adult, child caregivers often state their childhood experiences were a blessing in disguise. Many of the strengths they exhibit as an adult were developed by caring for a parent as a child.

However, the negative consequences of growing up in this type of environment is that anxiety is interwoven into all our thoughts and actions. I am forever on alert for the next issue I need to fix. I never feel completely at ease or safe, even as an adult.

A therapist once told me to envision my "safe place" whenever I felt overwhelmed, or I felt a panic attack was about to strike. She provided examples such as being at home in my favorite room, or being at a favorite vacation spot, or perhaps even being with someone instead of at a particular location. I remember going home feeling defeated. My husband asked what was wrong, and I had to admit to him (and myself), I do not have a "safe place." I never feel safe. I don't fear things happening to me; I anticipate them happening to me eventually.

Transforming the Broken Childhood

Retraining ourselves is part of the journey to a healthy and joyful life. As a young adult, many child caregivers, including myself, see education and work as a means to escape. So, I was the first in my family to graduate from college. I strive to not only meet the expectations of my employers, but to exceed them. My professional career allows me to be self-sufficient. In my mind, this enables me to keep my escape hatch open.

A participant of the study explained this desire to escape through success by stating,

> I was always mature, I was switched on, I can see that has been negative in a lot of ways, because I am so anxious and, that I can't relax. But I do see it as a big positive too, that I've just never stopped so I have achieved lots.

Unfortunately, an unintended consequence of constantly seeking success is being caught in the perfectionist whirlwind. (We'll explore that topic in another chapter.)

Remember the transferring the distress theme? Many times, the confusion that surrounded why a parent was ill leads the child to blame themselves for the illness. To deal with this misplaced guilt, child caregivers often take on additional responsibilities to help. More time is spent on activities associated with being an adult instead of activities associated with childhood. This desire to minimize the guilt leads to the never-ending need to constantly transform oneself into a better version.

Connected

As I reviewed each theme, emotions and memories of my childhood came rushing forward. I had neatly filed away many of these emotions without truly processing them. Who cares, trauma and betrayal, transferring distress, duck weaving and staying safe, growing myself up, and transforming a broken childhood seemed to illustrate my childhood. Realizing my connection to the themes was both comforting and frightening. All those emotions I dismissed as a child were valid. I wasn't being a "baby," I was trying to make sense of a difficult situation, and I wasn't alone. Others had faced the same challenges. That was comforting. Processing the emotions and realizing the effects of being raised in an environment charged with anxiety was the frightening part.

Think about your experiences in childhood. Can you relate to these themes? Maybe you experienced other situations that impacted you. The important thing is to remember what actually occurred. Then, take time to process the emotions associated with these memories. I cannot stress enough the importance of allowing yourself to feel without guilt. Successfully caring for a family member also requires taking care of yourself. Emotions, good and bad, are a part of our lives. Do not dismiss them. Acknowledge your feelings and then move forward. This will lead to a healthier, happier life for you and your family.

FRAGMENTS

"Through [skillful and godly] wisdom a house [a life, a home, a family] is built, and by understanding it is established [on a sound and good foundation]."

– Proverbs 24:3

Although I'm not sure my mother ever told me the entire story of how her anxiety began, I've pieced together what I believe to have happened. It is not unusual for parents to shield children from the reason why a mental illness condition exists. With anxiety, it is often related to a traumatic event that the parent does not want to share with the child.

My brothers are 17 months apart in age. My mother was able to resume normal activities after her first traumatic birth experience. However, during the birth of my second brother, she became hysterical and had to be sedated. She doesn't remember anything about the birthing experience. Sometime after this event (I'm not sure whether it was months or years), and possibly before I was born (again, not sure), my mother had a "nervous breakdown." I have no details of what exactly happened, but my mother was placed in a hospital for several days and was not allowed to have contact with family members.

Can you imagine how devastating it would be to be restricted from seeing your two (maybe three) small children for any length of time? My mother didn't share the details of her treatment – only that once she had "calmed down," she was able to return home. However, that is when the panic attacks began, and she was unable to stay home by herself or go to public places.

Some of my earliest memories are reading *Highlights* magazines with my mother and grandmother in a psychiatrist's waiting room. The nurse would call my mother's name, and she would go behind a door for about an hour. I would stay with my grandmother in the waiting room. I often asked why I couldn't go with my mother behind the door. My grandma would explain that my mother needed to have a private conversation with the doctor. She would appease me by finding magazines that I could read (which I loved reading!) and playing games with me.

After the hour lapsed, my mother would reappear, and we would head to the car. My mother never talked about the sessions. If I asked what she talked about with the doctor, she would answer, "Nothing."

After the visit to the psychiatrist, my mother would have several white pieces of paper that we would immediately take to the pharmacy. I didn't fully understand the connection at the time, but now I realize that my mother was on several medications to keep her "calm."

Looking back, I had a lot of responsibility placed on me as a child – responsibility that was given with little to no explanation. I am confident my parents were protecting me in their own way, but I was curious like any child would be. And I was resourceful. If I wasn't given a "why," I created one for the situation. In almost every case, my why was not accurate. Not even close. It's one thing to not have an answer as to why a situation exists. It's another to know and not share the information. Protection or not, trust begins to erode, and the real story is replaced with assumptions that are far worse than the reality.

In my journey to discovery, I came across another study completed by Jo Aldridge and Saul Becker. They collected information from forty families. Two aspects of their research drew my interest. First, the parents interviewed had experienced a past trauma which contributed to the onset of the mental health issue. That matched my mother's situation. Second, they also interviewed the children providing care to the parent. Having both the parent and child perspective gave a fuller picture of how the illness affected the entire family.

More Take-aways!

Below are a few items discussed in the study that resonated with my personal experiences. I believe it is important to share these take-aways to help illustrate the effect mental illness can have on families.

Moms Get a Bad Rap

Until the 1980's, moms that struggled with a mental illness were viewed as hysterical and trying to avoid their duties as a wife and mother. Many times, the care provided by the mother would be evaluated by social workers, leading to children being placed in foster care. During this time, research studies focused on the detriment a mother's health had on families with little information collected on the effect a father's mental health had on a family. Given this, why would a female seek help? If the shame of having a mental illness didn't deter you from getting help, the fear of losing your family definitely would stop you.

Kids Don't Count

Most studies in this era did not include the children caring for the parent. In fact, researchers believed child caregivers were uncommon. This was due to parents not completely sharing the dynamics of their family life. How would it be perceived if others knew that children were responsible for the care of a parent? The shame of not being able to function as a typical parent forced the parents to keep this information to themselves.

Mental Illness Has Many Friends

Mental illness always brings additional struggles to a family. Parents often face relationship problems which can lead to divorce. Luckily, my parents remained married, but I wouldn't have called it a loving relationship during my childhood years. My parents were in survival mode. I always feared my parents would get divorced. My fear wasn't based on whether they would continue to love me if separated, like most kids. I feared the responsibility of taking care of my mom alone.

Families battling mental illness often face financial difficulties. My mother was not able to work, and my father had to provide for our family. If he was sick or injured, our family did not have money for the bills. To bear that responsibility is extremely stressful. This leads to my next take-away.

Mental Illness Breeds Mental Illness

As a child, I always feared that I would have the same issues my mother faced. However, it's not just genetics that perpetuate mental illness within families. The everyday struggles of caring for a mentally ill family member creates an ongoing, traumatic experience that can cause an onset of any one of the illnesses defined earlier. Without the proper care and resources, depression, anxiety, phobias and other disorders continue to breed in families that battle mental illness every day.

Stigma Sucks

The stigma surrounding mental illness sucks the life out of individuals and families. I cannot stress this enough. The stigma society has traditionally placed on individuals suffering from a mental illness creates a layer of shame. That shame encompasses not only the individual but their family members as well. Parents hide their illness from family, friends, and neighbors to protect their children from ridicule. Spouses hide it from coworkers to protect their wife or husband and themselves from being ridiculed.

Where did this societal stigma originate? I don't recall a mentally ill monster rampaging the countryside in any history lessons. I believe it is formed from the fear of anything different. Physical ailments can be seen. Mental illness is invisible. In a world that demands diversity and inclusion, mental illness should lose its stigma and be treated as any other illness. It hasn't. Why? Actions speak louder than words. Until people come forward to share their personal challenges due to mental illness and others see there is no shame or stigma placed on them, the secret will be kept.

Child Caregivers Save the Day!

Professional caregivers often cannot respond to the needs of a patient in a timely manner. Relatives and friends may not live close enough to help or may not fully understand the illness their loved one is struggling to manage. Children of the mentally ill parent are in the best position to help. They have witnessed the daily struggles caused by the illness. They are available 24/7 to assist with care. Many times, the child has a calming effect on the parent just by being nearby. The care provided by children assists the parent in leading as close to a "normal" life as possible. The cost of a professional providing the same level of care would be astronomical.

Tell the Story

It's interesting that several articles on children caregivers state the children take on the role of the parent – role reversal. However, this study revealed it was more role adaptation than reversal.

My mom set the rules, held me accountable, and had the final say. She was Mom. I did not gain that power because I cared for her. Don't get me wrong. I tried on several occasions to exercise that power and was quickly put in my place! I did, however, adapt to her needs, and I carried out additional duties as needed. Those duties often resulted in fewer social opportunities with my peers and increased anxiety from being away from home.

One such example happened to me in high school. I was selected to represent my school at the state capital. This was a major honor, which required spending several nights away from home. Both my parents assured me they could accommodate my absence. Other family members would help out while I was away. Even so, I couldn't do it. I was so anxious, and I had no idea at the time why I feared leaving. I ultimately declined the opportunity to go and watched another classmate accept the honor. It broke my heart.

As a child, I never talked about my mother's illness with anyone, including my grandmother and aunt who helped my family on many occasions. It was just "accepted," and everyone cautiously navigated around it. I didn't ask questions or complain because it felt like I would be disrespecting my mom.

This study revealed that most child caregivers interviewed kept quiet about their family situation because they didn't trust anyone to understand. I felt that way. It's not enough to talk about mental illness. Children need avenues to discuss their situation and work out the emotions associated with the responsibility given to them. Until we talk about how caring affects our lives, and are reassured that negative consequences will not occur, healing for the whole family will not happen.

The silence, the secrets and the worry unknowingly eat away at a child's self-confidence, and anxiety follows. Caring for a mentally ill family member affects a person's view of the outside world. Doubt, mistrust, and always waiting for the next situation that needs to be handled drive child caregivers to be over-achievers with issues. I know. I have these tendencies engrained into my personality, and I had no idea until now.

Child caregivers need to unite. Open discussions on experiences and feelings should be encouraged. Instead of trying to remove caregivers from the situation, support should be given to help them understand their family members' illness, and they should be empowered to participate in possible care solutions for their family member. If I could have one request granted from parents of child caregivers, it would be this – tell the back story, and let the caregiver help create the future. Piece the fragments together and create the whole picture for your loved ones.

TRAUMA OR TRAINING

"My grace is sufficient for you; for power is being perfected in weakness. Therefore, I will all the more gladly boast in my weaknesses, so that the power of Christ may dwell in me."
– 2 Corinthians 12:9

The trauma my mother experienced during childbirth was not addressed. The stigma of mental illness, the belief that anxiety was just nervous behavior that could easily be overcome by willpower, and the lack of resources to continue care all contributed to not having the resources available to help my family. The ongoing care I provided to my mother was in essence the trauma I experienced in childhood. Yes, trauma.

To me, trauma is an extremely harmful situation that a person has no control over. Pictures of being held at gunpoint, stranded in extreme weather, physical abuse by a parent, spouse or other family member are all traumatic experiences. My mother facing death while giving birth was a traumatic experience. However, there is also emotional trauma that is the result of extraordinarily stressful events that damage your sense of security.

Everywhere I searched for information on anxiety and how it affects families, trauma popped up. Articles on how not to traumatize your children if you were raised in a home with mental illness were all over the place. Professionals encouraging adults raised by a mentally ill parent to seek counselling that focused on overcoming trauma was a common theme in the articles. I was so confused! I didn't feel like a victim.

The truth is my mother's unaddressed trauma created ongoing emotional trauma for me that affected my adult life. That's a hard truth to accept. It's not about placing blame. It's more about understanding what happened so that it doesn't happen again. I need to recognize the negative effects of my youth so that I do not carry forward the misconceptions learned during this period.

It's important to remember that a young caregiver is still a child. Yes, due to circumstances, these caregivers are mature for their age, have developed a deep sense of empathy for others, and handle stressful situations with grace. But they are still children, under construction, needing support, care and guidance.

During my childhood, it was often hard to determine if I was loved. My parents provided shelter, food and all the basic needs of a developing child. However, they both faced daily challenges in providing those basic needs to us. Stress, hurt feelings and frustration created a difficult environment in which to raise children and have a healthy marriage. The environment shifted from a loving atmosphere to a hurtful one – within minutes – at any given time. This is difficult to understand as a child. Survival mode kicks in, and you learn to adapt quickly to whatever environment is presented. However, the question as to whether you are wanted and loved remains.

For me, I was needed by my parents. Therefore, I believed I was wanted. Unfortunately, a healthy relationship at any age should not be based on whether an individual fills a need. Scripture states that our worth is not in the work we complete, but the love we demonstrate to one another. I believe this is true in our relationship with God and in our relationship with one another.

So, is it trauma or training young caregivers experience? It's both. Learning how to deal with demanding situations trains young caregivers to be resilient. On the flip side, watching parents react anxiously in certain circumstances teaches children to respond in the same way. It's like a yo-yo; one experience teaches a positive behavior, and the next experience teaches a negative behavior. Unfortunately, the child caregiver doesn't have the time or luxury to stop and analyze each situation.

The young caregivers' focus must remain on maintaining an environment that keeps everyone at peace with one another. The constant yo-yo environment creates the ongoing trauma which in turn creates the opportunities for training. The stress felt by the family is overwhelming and continues forward in a never-ending cycle.

Most of my life, I did not recognize the negative behaviors I learned during my childhood. I made excuses or denied my childhood had any negative effect on me. And the concept that my childhood was a traumatic experience for me never crossed my mind. Unfortunately, whether recognized or not, these behaviors, both good and bad, have a way of surfacing.

As an adult, I tend to "play down" experiences. As babies, my sons each had medical issues that had to be overcome. For example, my oldest had a kidney infection when he was three years old. This is uncommon for a boy. Luckily, our pediatrician was thorough in his care. He requested tests to determine the cause of his high fever and intense pain, and from these tests, the infection was revealed.

I remember the nurse telling me not to worry, as only a small percentage of tests came back positive for kidney issues. Immediate dread washed over my body. I'd heard that several times beginning with my pregnancies. All the tests given during your pregnancy to identify possible health concerns, such as gestational diabetes, all came back positive. And conversations with health professionals explaining the tests were performed out of an abundance of caution and rarely came back positive mirrored my conversation at the pediatrician's office.

So yes, my son's test was positive and additional testing, images and specialist appointments followed. Ultimately, we found the cause for the infection, and we were able to monitor the situation during the next four years. The end result was that his kidneys remained healthy and developed normally.

Fast forward ten years, and I am once again in the pediatrician's office. It was time for my son's annual physical. He had not visited the doctor during the entire year. His doctor remarked on how wonderful that was for our family. My response (which was typical for me) included the usual "Yes, but we have nothing to complain about. Our son's health issues have all been manageable." The doctor stopped entering information into the computer system and stared straight at me in disbelief. He stated, "You have been through a lot over the years – more than most families."

I remember telling my husband that night how surprised I was by the doctor's statement. My husband said, "Why did that surprise you? We have been through a lot!" It surprised me because as a child I was trained to remain calm and not over-dramatize any situation. If I did, it could have negative consequences at home. I carried this "training" into my adult life. Although it benefited me when dealing with emergencies or stressful situations, internally, it was not healthy.

During my much-needed counseling sessions following my father's death, my therapist told me she could tell I was very resilient. A positive trait I learned during my childhood. Together, we discovered tools I could use daily to move forward and process the waves of emotions that hit me when my father died. I really felt like I could handle life in a healthier way and move the sessions to an as needed basis instead of meeting regularly.

As we discussed this, the therapist asked if there were any other items I wanted to discuss. And there was one. I had a fear unrelated to my childhood, or so I thought, that I wanted to tackle. I have a fear of driving on major highways. Any time I try to drive on a busy highway with multiple lanes, I have a panic attack. For several years. I had a lengthy commute to work. During this commute, I witnessed major car accidents almost daily. Many times, I would be stuck on the highway for an hour or more due to these accidents. It was horrible. I believed the panic attacks were related to these experiences.

After sharing my fear, the therapist just sat quietly for a moment, then asked, "Did you have to drive your mother places when you first started driving?" Strange question, but I answered it. "Of course, me getting my license actually provided a bit of freedom for the two of us." The therapist then asked, "How did your mom react when you drove her to different places?" My response, "She was always very anxious telling me to slow down, watch the other cars, and to be careful." That's when the light bulb went off in my head – my mom taught me to be nervous in traffic. In essence, wiring me to equate traffic to fear. Even though I had come to terms with my childhood experiences, the effects were far from over.

Time to Heal

I started questioning all my behaviors at this point. I was curious to know if I was acting in a healthy manner or creating chaos for myself or others. How did my past effect my present? I came across a book written by Nadine Burke Harris, M.D.

In *The Deepest Well – Healing the Long-Term Effects of Childhood Adversity*, Dr. Harris applies research from a study completed by Dr. Vincent Felitti, Dr. Robert Anda, and colleagues to uncover how adversity manifest in not only a person's emotional well-being, but causes physical ailments as well. The study examined the link between childhood adversity and health outcomes. Research inspired by this study has discovered that individuals who experienced adverse childhood experiences have a greater risk for developing serious diseases in adulthood.

Dr. Harris echoed other researchers, stating a family pays a price by keeping silent about a family member's traumatic experiences. She notes talking openly about these experiences has not been the common practice for families. This leads children to believe they are the cause of the family's problems.

Although parents believe they are protecting the child by not sharing what created the stressful home environment, the opposite is true. Not talking about past events is actually more traumatic to the child. Dr. Harris emphasizes in her writings that the most important thing is to recognize what the problem is and face it. That includes acknowledging the past events that contributed to the challenges faced in the present.

In addition, Dr. Harris discovered that children exposed to traumatic events over a period of time will develop overactive stress responses. The overwhelming feeling that I must always be on guard for the next problem to arise is an example of this type of response. It takes stress to a new level that is toxic to the body. This is also referred to as toxic stress.

Overactive stress response left unmanaged can contribute to developing serious health problems. Ironically, most people who are wired to have overactive stress responses do not realize it. Honestly, before reading Dr. Harris' book, I had never heard of it! For this reason, lifetimes are spent chasing symptoms with no real answer to the cause of the ailments.

I have a personal example from several years ago. My husband and I were expecting our first child, and I had a miscarriage. For my family, this was an anomaly. The women on my mother's and father's sides of the family had healthy pregnancies well into their forties. Miscarriages did not happen. Everyone was in shock.

To make matters worse, even though the baby was no longer vital, my body continued to produce hormones as though it was. Due to this, a surgery was performed to remove the fetus from my body. Based on my body's reactions, my doctor was convinced I had suffered either a partial molar pregnancy, or my body was treating the growing fetus as a virus in the body and attacking it. The likelihood of having future successful pregnancies was slim.

As with most medical conditions, additional testing was required to confirm the diagnosis. My husband and I were devastated. There was no family history of these types of conditions and no way to prevent it from happening in the future. Several weeks later, the results came in. Guess what? I did not have either condition. The doctors couldn't explain why my body responded to the pregnancy in that manner. Three years later, I became pregnant with our oldest son and had no complications.

Was this medical experience related to my overactive stress response developed during my childhood? Perhaps. I can share several other medical oddities I have experienced that ended with the same response from my medical providers. I would have the symptoms of a major illness, and tests would follow only to discover I did not have the illness.

What if Dr. Harris is right? Recent studies show improving your physical health has a positive impact on your mental health. Exercise is commonly used to combat depression and anxiety. Stress can be reduced by eating a healthy diet. So why wouldn't it make sense that by taking care of our mental health our physical health would also improve? Why is there a distinction between the two? People should take care of their whole selves, mental and physical combined.

It really is simple. Take care of yourself from a holistic viewpoint and both your body and mind will benefit. So where do we start? Dr. Harris' research discovered six things a person can do to reduce the effect of toxic stress. Interestingly, these six things are also recommended to improve a person's physical health.

1. Sleep – You need seven to eight hours of sleep a night, no excuses.
2. Exercise – any type of exercise done for an hour a day will reduce the effect of toxic stress and strengthen your physical health. Start slow and build up to an hour. I started walking for 15 minutes on Saturday and Sunday. I increased the time by 5 minutes until I reached the hour mark. Now I'm trying to increase the number of days. Even though I haven't reached the hour a day goal, I already feel stronger both mentally and physically. You will too.
3. Nutrition – In the past, I related nutrition to dieting. My negative self-image probably influenced this perception. However, being mindful of nutrition simply means be mindful of what you put in your body. A great place to start learning about nutrition is MyPlate.gov. It provides

an overview of healthy eating that is simple to apply. You may have to do a bit of research, but it is important to discover what your body needs and to establish eating habits that support those needs.

4. Mindfulness – I relate mindfulness to self-care. Listen to what your body is trying to tell you. If you feel overwhelmed, take a "time-out" and find a quiet place to regain your focus. Low on energy? Maybe your eating or sleeping habits need to be adjusted. Be mindful of what you need to remain strong, mentally and physically. And this should be done throughout the day – not scheduled for once a week!

5. Mental Health – Breaking the anxiety cycle means addressing strongholds on our own perception of mental illness. Watching my mother struggle should be all the motivation I need to seek out help for any mental illnesses I may experience. However, I also have learned behaviors engrained in me from watching my mother handle her anxiety. Although I knew counseling would and has helped me, every time I went to an appointment, I had a voice inside me screaming that I should be strong enough to handle this on my own. What I realized was the stigma of mental illness had been buried within me. The only choice, if I want to break this cycle, is to stand up to the lies this stigma represents. And I encourage you to do the

same. If you feel overwhelmed, seek professional counseling. There is no shame in asking for help. For child caregivers, it is important to find trauma focused interventions. Ok, I know your first response is probably, "Whatever." It was definitely my first response, but I did it anyway. And I am extremely glad I did. It is critical for a counselor to understand your past isn't just about the mental illness your family battled, but the daily emotional stress that was placed on you as a child caregiver. Trauma focused counseling will help you focus on the whole picture, your whole story, and find ways to turn unhealthy behaviors into healthy ones.

6. Healthy Relationships – This is so important. Later we will discuss healthy boundaries which help to build healthy relationships. For now, understand that healthy relationships do not trigger stress responses. Yes, we all have "triggers" that send us over the edge when it comes to stress and being anxious. Being in a relationship that constantly triggers these responses is not healthy for you or the other person. If you have relationships in which you are constantly hiding things from other people in your life, you have unhealthy relationships. Remember, toxic stress feeds on secrecy and the shame secrets create.

So, is toxic stress the cause for all our health concerns? No, but it is a plausible explanation for some of them. Always seek medical advice for symptoms that cause you concern, and share your trauma experience with your doctor. All of this together may help you get the proper treatment for your symptoms. Recognizing the potential effect overactive stress response has on your health and taking action to minimize its occurrence, is critical to your health.

For me, learning this information gave me a new view of myself. Picture the scene from the movie, *Dr. Strange*, in which the Ancient One pushes Dr. Strange's spirit out of his physical body to demonstrate there is more to him than just his physical self. Once I took a step outside of my "known" self and openly looked at my entire self – physical and mental in the past and present – a complete picture evolved.

To be healthy, you must consider your whole self. Compartmentalizing yourself as a protective measure only weakens the whole. You can't hide away the parts of your life that cause pain – just like you can't permanently hide away parts of your physical body. To heal, you must be all in: mind, body and spirit. This is true for everyone. The goal is to learn how to support healthy behaviors regardless of the situation. You are in control.

Beauty From Ashes

Toxic stress penetrates individuals, and it can leave lasting effects, good and bad. The side effects of toxic stress are not based on whether a person is "strong" or not. It's a reaction to an abnormal situation. As an adult, it's important to understand this and to not be ashamed of any health issues that arise. As a child, experiencing toxic stress is a defining element of development. Many children develop unmatched resiliency, a deep sense of empathy, and a natural ability to care and protect others.

In the "Fractured Journey" study previously discussed in the "Life of a Caregiver" chapter, researchers discovered that many youth caregivers experienced posttraumatic growth. This type of positive personal growth occurs despite the exposure to trauma. Specifically, psychological growth such as positive reevaluation of self, greater appreciation for relationships, and revised values and beliefs occurred. Even though the participants of this study shared a deep sense of alienation, social neglect, inadequate support from adults, and stigma from outsiders, all felt a need to redefine their lives as adults. Changes made by participants resulted in a positive outlook on life, with participants developing a powerful sense of empathy and emotional maturity. A common goal was to overcome adversity, re-define self and build a better life for future generations. All recognized that although they loved their mentally ill parent, as an adult, boundaries had to be maintained to protect their own mental well-being.

I love this quote from the study:

> The primary narrative of these seven participants is one of hope; that, despite years of childhood trauma, it is possible to re-define self. Through the development of secure pseudo-attachment relationships, goal-oriented behavior across the various domains and purposeful meaning-making and reflection, these participants deterred adversity, forgave their parents' betrayal, and fostered a self, worthy of love, acceptance, and success.

The past does not define you. God made you to be a unique individual. Be who you were meant to be and create a life full of hope.

Embrace the Past

It's not about overcoming our childhood but embracing it. I know from experience this is harder than it sounds. I'd love to share that this is a "one and done" process, but it's not. For me, it's a daily challenge and usually involves the simplest things. I'll give you an example.

I made an appointment with a new dermatologist for my routine wellness exam. The dermatologist's staff sent me a packet of forms to complete prior to my visit. It contained all the usual forms, including a request for past medical histories on me and my extended family. I'm sure you are familiar with this one. The questions usually revolve around who in my family has had cancer, asthma, high blood pressure, and so on. However, nestled in these normal questions was one asking if anyone in my family had experienced a nervous breakdown. That was new. I hesitated and then marked the box labeled "no." Then I heard a voice inside say, "Really? You're writing a book about sharing your story and owning your story, and you marked no?!"

Okay, I did change it to "yes," but a wave of anxiety swept over me as I marked the correct box. My secret was out! And guess what happened? There were no alarms that went off in the office, I wasn't escorted to the "special" room at the medical facility, and no one even pointed at me. What did happen is that I provided my doctor my whole medical history so that he could provide better direction for my medical care.

I will spend the rest of my life trying to purposely view the world from a healthy perspective and respond with healthy behaviors. Ongoing improvement – doesn't that fit perfectly into our youth caregiver profile? Marking "yes" on the medical form was a victory in this area for me. We must find the courage to face our past in order to have the power to transform not only our health, but the health of those around us.

One final thought on healing comes from a quote by Dr. Harris. "I believe that when we each find the *courage* to look this problem in the face, we will have the power to transform not only our health, but our world."

ART OF BEING YOU

Transform

YOU ARE ENOUGH

"Have I not commanded you? Be strong and courageous! Do not be terrified or dismayed, for the Lord your God is with you wherever you go."

– Joshua 1:9

I have owned my story, discovered the truth about my mother's illness and found others that have faced similar challenges. Where does that leave me? I want a healthy, joyful life, but I'm not sure what that even looks like for me. It's time to dig deeper.

Going through the process to discover the difference between healthy behaviors and negative behaviors is difficult and feels as though it is never-ending. Hopefully, you will begin this process much earlier than when I started. But know, it will be challenging nonetheless. Remember, you are not alone on this path of capturing a healthy and joyful life. Talk about your struggles with those you trust have your best interest at heart, share your experiences with others that have similar struggles, and have a continual conversation with God for guidance and support.

To battle everyday challenges, I seek protection from God. Psalm 91:4 reads, "He will cover you and completely protect you with His pinions, and under His wings you will find refuge; His faithfulness is a shield and a wall". Do you know what a pinion is? I didn't. It is the outer part of a bird's wing that they use in flight to guide them. Understanding this scripture helped me realize that God will protect and steer me in the right direction every day. I do not have to fear the future or plan it out to be successful. If I trust Him, God will continue to direct my path to success.

The Why

I know what you are thinking. I had the same question. If God is our safe place, and He is in control, why did He allow this to happen to me? Why didn't God heal my mother so she could take care of me and my brothers? Why didn't God at least protect me from developing unhealthy behaviors? The answer is revealed in John 10:10.

> The thief comes only to steal and kill and destroy. I have come that they may have life, and have it to the full.

God has blessed us with free will. We have the choice to let the devil or "thief" steal, kill and destroy our hope through difficult situations or to stand firm in the belief that God will help us to prevail. God didn't create the situations that framed my childhood. He gave my mother the free will to choose to trust in Him or to remain captive to her fear. I have a choice too. I can let the unhealthy behaviors I learned as a child define and control me, or I can break the anxiety cycle and trust God to help me adapt to new behaviors.

My mother taught me to have a strong Christian faith and encouraged me to have a close relationship with God. I am forever grateful for this. I do not blame my mother for not exercising her faith to overcome her anxiety. No one really understood her medical condition. Due to ignorance and out of love, my family took care of my mother, so she didn't have to face her fears. That changed when my father passed away. Once she made the decision to battle her fears, God gave her the courage to overcome years of anxiety and to be able to care for herself.

Own Your Story

I shared my story in the beginning for a reason. I wanted you to see the whole picture of who I am. To truly understand who you are, you must first understand where you have been. Own your story – the good, the bad and the ugly. Do not be afraid to face those hidden parts of your past and share your experiences with others. You will be stronger for it.

Hiding the parts of my past that I thought others would view as negative was exhausting. Half the time, I didn't even realize what I was doing. I always wondered why being around new people or attending a networking event physically exhausted me. Now I know. Constantly hiding parts of myself and analyzing the environment to determine if I had been successful at hiding my past is hard! I realize now, being my whole self is so much easier. Yes, I had to work through my fear of rejection, but that's actually easier than keeping parts of myself locked away. I discovered that my fear was much greater than the actual rejection I have faced when sharing my whole self with others.

So, what is your story? The real story. It's neither good or bad, the events are no one's fault and there is no shame. It's simply your perception of the events that occurred in your past. I bet if you asked my brothers about the events in my story, their versions would be different from mine and from one another's. That's okay. People experience events differently. The storyline may be similar, but how it affected the spectators will differ based on their own values, experiences, and points of view. My story is not my brothers' stories. It is not my parents' story. It is mine. That's what you need to discover for yourself – your personal story. It doesn't have to meet anyone's approval. It doesn't have to be factually perfect (for my perfectionist buddies out there). It only needs to represent your point of view, your perspective.

In *Gifts of Imperfection*, Brené Brown shares that owning our story can be difficult, but not as difficult as spending a lifetime running away from it. Dr. Brown is a research professor at the University of Houston. Her research work focuses on the effects of vulnerability, courage, worthiness and shame. Through her work, she discovered that individuals who live life with courage, compassion and connection experience joy and peace throughout their life. This "wholehearted" style of living requires you to believe you are worthy, you are enough. To be wholehearted, you must know who you really are; you must know your story.

I strongly encourage you to take the time and write out your story. It will be hard. Remembering what happened is the easy part. It's the emotions you will be faced with as you write the words on the paper that hurt. That's why it's so important to write it out. It forces you to face the emotions that have been bottled up inside you for so long. It helps identify where your "stinking thinking" (as Joyce Meyer says) resides and where unhealthy behaviors may exist. Identifying these areas are the first step to a healthier you. It hurts, but at the same time, it is freeing. So, I ask again. What is your *real* story?

Get to Work!

The remaining sections of this chapter represent the areas that were particularly hard for me to overcome – my personal rewire sessions. Hopefully, this will spark ideas on how you can become aware of these (or other) unhealthy behaviors and recognize that additional effort is needed to ensure your actions and thoughts remain healthy.

> Romans 5:3-5 offers us the following inspiration:
> And not only this, but let us exult in our sufferings and rejoice in our hardships, knowing that hardship produces patient endurance; and endurance, proven character; and proven character, hope and confident assurance. Such hope never disappoints us, because God's love has been abundantly poured out within our hearts through the Holy Spirit who was given to us.

Even though facing these unhealthy behaviors is difficult, it's not impossible with God's help. By overcoming these struggles, we will emerge with strong healthy traits that will enable us to be confident and full of hope.

Vulnerability

I imagined vulnerability to be like a daytime television show where guests are invited to share their life problems while a live audience tells the guests how messed up they really are. No thank you. In fact, being vulnerable with other people felt foreign to me. I already feel like I'm not worthy, why would I showcase my weaknesses? That's the point, though, isn't it? To connect with others, we must be vulnerable and share who we truly are inside. Otherwise, we will never form a real connection.

You hear a lot about authenticity or being "authentic." What exactly does that mean? The Merriam-Webster dictionary defines authentic as real or genuine, not copied or false. To be authentic is to be true to yourself, the real you. You are not what others expect you to be, not the world's version of perfect, but your true self, which encompasses your strengths and weaknesses all in one.

This seems simple enough, but it's not for a child caregiver. The expectation has always been to be what others need, not who you are. In fact, I'm not sure I fully know who the real Jannette is at this point. Maybe that's why it is so hard to be vulnerable. I hid a part of my life to protect my family, which meant I also hid a part of myself. That goes against the concept of vulnerability, which requires putting your whole self out there for all to see.

Vulnerability seemed so scary to me. The mention of it made me nauseous. I'm serious. But my perception of vulnerability was distorted. My initial thought of vulnerability was tied to weakness. The basic definition of being vulnerable is capable of being damaged. Now I am being told that to be authentic, you must be vulnerable. So, does that mean I have to demonstrate I am fragile to be myself? Who wants that?!

Being fragile is not in a child caregiver's vocabulary. In order to care for my mother, I had to set my feelings aside. Don't get me wrong, I still felt anguish, despair, and frustration, but I couldn't dwell on these emotions if I wanted to accomplish the actions needed to keep my home environment stable. However, dismissing these feelings created yet another barrier inside me that prevented me from connecting with others. Yes, I felt these emotions, but instead of sorting through them, I ignored them. I thought if I allowed myself to feel these "negative" emotions I was allowing myself to be weak. I wanted to be self-sufficient.

What I didn't understand is that taking the time to allow yourself to process emotions actually provides strength. Bottling up emotions only weakens your ability to feel and creates anxiety, which I did not want or need. This is another reason being vulnerable is so important. If you accept your weaknesses and allow yourself to share your vulnerabilities, hiding these emotions becomes unnecessary. The anxiety of keeping yet another secret goes away when you allow yourself to be vulnerable with others.

In her book, *Daring Greatly*, Brené Brown sums it up the best. She stated that the fear of being vulnerable holds you back. Trying to micro-manage situations and people is a shield to prevent feeling vulnerable. This shield only keeps you from knowing yourself and letting others know you. It requires that you stay small and quiet behind it so as not to draw attention to your imperfections and vulnerabilities.

So where do we go from here? I believe discovering and sharing that you have no idea how to be vulnerable is, in itself, being vulnerable. I'll pause while you mull that over. Think about it. Being vulnerable is being real with others. I have layers of protective behaviors developed to keep people from discovering my past. If I admit I have issues, I'm being honest about myself, gently removing one layer of my protective barrier. Learning to be vulnerable begins with simple steps.

The point is all humans are capable of being damaged. In fact, most of us have been damaged physically or emotionally in some manner. So why pretend we are perfect – or even close to it – and keep people at a distance to protect our secret? To connect with one another, we must accept that we are all on the same playing field. We are who God made us to be. That is enough. Vulnerability is the art of showing the world your imperfect self. Relax, and instead of trying to be everything to everyone, just be yourself.

Perfectionist

Perfection was not a personal goal for me, it was a way of life. If I didn't receive the top score in class, if I wasn't the best piano player at the recital, if I didn't get the lead in a school play, I was a complete failure in my eyes. And to be clear, I am not perfect. In fact, there isn't a soul on this earth that can claim to be perfect. That didn't matter. If I didn't believe I could be the best at (fill in the blank), I wouldn't even attempt it. Failure was not an option. I realize now that I have missed out on so many opportunities in my life because I allowed perfectionism to rule me.

Do you find yourself having patience for others but not yourself? I expect a great deal from myself. If I am not timely, if I don't complete everything on my daily task list, if I don't exceed expectations (not meet but exceed), I feel like I should have done more. This feeling is part of the perfectionist pitfall. Nothing is ever enough. It is also a side effect of being a former child caregiver.

Failure is not an option for a child caregiver. As a child, I believed if I didn't help my mother, she would become sick and possibly die. Dramatic, but as we discussed earlier, if children do not understand or know the whole story behind a family member's illness, they will make up their own version.

Remember the themes discovered in the study we discussed in "The Life of a Caregiver" chapter? The study revealed that child caregivers often blame themselves for their parent's illness. This guilt, or shame, is what drives a child caregiver to take on additional responsibilities. Many times, this shame continues into a child caregiver's adult life, morphing into a belief that success somehow makes up for the perceived failure of not being able to help the parent overcome their illness. Wanting to be successful, in itself, is not a negative behavior. However, when you allow your perceived success to dictate how you view yourself, that is when perfectionism begins to negatively impact your life.

Brené Brown provides the perfect visual example of perfectionism. She compares it to a twenty-ton shield that perfectionists lug around to protect themselves. However, this heavy accessory actually prevents perfectionists from taking flight. Imagining this perfectionist shield tied around my body helped me realize how the expectations I place on myself really tie me down. Being perfect is an unattainable goal. The goal should be focused on being the best version of yourself as possible. That is enough.

Unfortunately, I've lugged that twenty-ton shield around for most of my life. I thought to be accepted I had to be perfect. I had to look perfect, act perfect and have the perfect solution to everyone's problems. I thought this was necessary for people to accept me, secrets and all. What a recipe for disaster! There is no earthly way to meet this expectation. I basically set myself up for failure. My fear of disappointment and the unrealistic performance pressure I placed on myself destroyed what little hope I had and replaced it with self-doubt.

Perfectionist tendencies can be positive or negative, depending on how you view success. If you strive to do your best and push yourself to achieve goals, that is not necessarily unhealthy. It's when you believe your worth is tied to whether you achieve your goals that negative perfectionism develops. Be mindful of the motivation behind the goals you set for yourself. If at any time you feel guilty or shameful because you didn't meet your or others' expectations, step back and reevaluate what is driving you. You do not have to be perfect to be accepted. That is a lie that holds you back from finding your true potential. To be worthy only requires that you try. That's it.

People Pleaser

A side effect of being a perfectionist is being a people pleaser. I'll give you a moment to recover from that last statement. I cannot express how hard it was for me to accept this. Brené Brown discusses this relationship in her work. The first time I read her explanation on how perfectionists are people pleasers at heart, I quietly sat the book down on my table and refused to continue reading it! Seriously, I walked by that book for several days, each time looking at it in disgust. I am a Generation Xer at heart. My personal anthem was centered around being an independent thinker and being self-sufficient. I wore combat boots in college – and did not care what others thought of me. People pleaser…please.

Fortunately, my curiosity got the best of me. I eventually read the rest of the book, and it actually made sense. (I still don't like it.) I have always placed my value on accomplishments. Who am I accomplishing these tasks for? People. If I perform well, I receive the acceptance of others. Why didn't I see this before now?

A few years later, I took a behavioral test at work designed to help identify what work environment is most effective for me. Once again, I was identified as a people pleaser. Although in this context it wasn't a negative characteristic, I took it as one. Were my actions based on what others thought of me? I knew I was a perfectionist. I will own that. But in my mind, being a perfectionist meant being an over-achiever, not people pleaser.

Have you ever heard the song "Purple People Eater"? It was popular in the late fifties. My parents had a music collection that included the song. I remember singing along to the song and laughing at the thought of a one-eyed, one horn purple people eater. After learning perfectionists are also people pleasers, an image of me as a one eyed, one horned, purple people *pleaser* popped into my head. People screaming as they run away from me, while I follow them yelling, "I only want to please you!" A bit dramatic, but you get the point.

Looking back, I can see where being a child caregiver promoted this unhealthy behavior in me. I had to be patient with my mother; she was constantly battling her own fears and anxiety. If I pushed her too hard, she would struggle. By pushing her, I am referring to making her uncomfortable in everyday situations. For example, I had daily chores that had to be accomplished. The chores were common tasks most kids had to do to help out: doing laundry, cleaning dishes and dusting furniture. If I failed to complete my tasks according to my mother's expectations, her entire day would be affected. If I argued that it was unfair that I had to help clean, she'd get upset, and that would negatively affect her entire day. If my mother's expectations were not met, anxiety would overwhelm her making her incapable of handling anything. And when that happened, I had nowhere to go.

If, however, I did everything according to my mother's plan and helped her stay on course, less stress followed. So, in essence, I was trained that meeting other people's expectations will keep everything in my world calm.

It's okay to want to please others with our actions. It becomes a problem when this desire becomes unbalanced in our lives. If being perfect or having others' acceptance is so important that your happiness is dependent on it, it's a problem. Joyce Meyer explains it best in her book, *Authentically, Uniquely You.* If you are a people pleaser, you have unrealistic expectations. You cannot meet every person's expectation. And you definitely can't do it if you desire to meet God's expectations as well.

As a caregiver, we had to set aside our own needs, but as adults we need to focus on ourselves. Otherwise, our life will not be balanced. There is only so much you can give until you break.

Focusing on your own health is not self-centered. It's necessary if you want to continue to help others. Notice, I used the word *help*, not *please*.

The following is a quote from Joyce Meyer's book:

> ...people-pleasers wrongly assume responsibility for other people's emotional reactions, such as anger, unhappiness, or disappointment, and they often adjust their own behavior to whatever will keep the other person happy. In doing this, they are allowing those people to control them with their emotions....We must be beware of having a false sense of responsibility.

Ouch! My peacemaking ability is really derived from a need to be a people pleaser. The comment on having a false sense of responsibility hit home for me as well. I am constantly trying to take care of situations for anyone and everyone. Even when I'm driving, I always consider how any action I take such as switching lanes, speeding up, slowing down will affect the cars around me. It's a lot to consider, and it can be stressful! I have a false sense of being responsible for their safety. In reality, if I focus on taking care of myself and let others take care of themselves, everyone is in a better position. I am one person. I can't control everything, but God can.

Joyce Meyer goes on to say that people pleasers are dishonest because they never tell people what they genuinely want or need. Ouch again! If I'm being honest, I was taught as a caregiver that pleasing my mother provided the care she needed. And I applied this lesson to every relationship I had thereafter. Looking back, I see how others' reactions have determined how I acted, what action I took, and how I related to them. I am constantly worrying about how my actions affect others that I forget to focus on what is right for me. That is not healthy.

So how do you get out of the people-pleasing business? It's not easy. Those who have benefited from your actions will want it to continue and will most likely pressure you to stay the course. The key is to establish healthy boundaries. When asked to do something for another person, take a moment and determine if you sincerely want to help or whether you feel pressure to do so. Remember, there should be a healthy balance between helping others and helping yourself. If a request falls outside what is healthy for you, you have to say no. As you define the boundaries, it sometimes helps to offer alternatives to those that want your assistance. We'll take a closer look at establishing boundaries in a later chapter.

I came across this scripture in 1 Thessalonians that reiterates people-pleasing is not in God's plan for us. It reads, "But just as we have been approved by God to be entrusted with the gospel, so we speak, not as to please people, but to please God who examines our hearts." Our actions should be based on what pleases God, not the world.

Pride and Self-Issues

An unexpected side effect of being a caregiver is pride. Yes, pride. Pride has many definitions, but for me it occurred when I felt happy after accomplishing a task better than anyone else. Here's an example: Even though I felt inadequate and like a failure on the inside, on the outside, I projected a calm demeanor to keep my surroundings peaceful. Classic caregiver tactic. And because I kept the peace so well, I received accolades from my parents, my teachers and my employers. These accolades made me feel better than other people. They made me feel more important. Pride.

It's important to understand that being prideful does not necessarily mean you are selfish. It is true, many times, prideful people are also selfish, thinking only of their own interests. However, being selfish is not an option for a child caregiver. The needs of our family member always trump our personal needs.

I did discover that there were other "self" issues besides selfishness that were causing unhealthy behaviors in my life. Many relate to the insecurity I felt as a child, and others I developed as defense mechanisms. It really doesn't matter when or why I developed the behaviors. What is important is to recognize the negative impact these behaviors have on my life and work to correct them.

I have issues surrounding self-analysis, self-consciousness, self-criticism, self-righteousness and self-sufficiency (to name a few). I tend to over analyze any mistakes I make (self-analysis). I am uncomfortable with my physical appearance (self-consciousness). I severely judge myself without providing the grace I would extend to others (self-criticism). I pride myself (there is that word again) in doing what is morally right which unconsciously leads to judging others who are not as "moral" or ethical as I am (self-righteousness). And finally, I am horrible at asking for help (self-sufficiency)!

This makes me sound like a monster! But the reality is that these behaviors reside quietly in my thoughts behind my walls of safety. So on the outside I appear to be happy and loving of everyone, but inside, these negative emotions are eating away at my happiness. All the negative focus on myself leaves extraordinarily little room for loving myself or others.

In order to take the first step towards right thinking, you must surrender control to God. God will make things right. He does not need your help. However, as a child caregiver, you are expected to take care of things. Failure to perform could negatively impact your family member's health. I must admit, trusting that God will handle the day-to-day responsibilities and relinquishing control to Him was scary to me. It seemed foreign to who I thought I was supposed to be. It just felt wrong.

1 Peter 5: 6-7 reminds us that if we humble ourselves to God and cast all our worries and cares to him, He will exalt us at the appropriate time. And considering He knows everything that has, is, and will happen, He's got it covered. The only reason we fail to let go is pride. My pride kept repeating, "If I am needed, I am wanted." But remember, our worth is not in what we produce (or do), it is in the love we show one another. Pride and other self-issues are like a heavy weight hanging around your neck, holding you down. Let go – God's got your back!

Love Yourself

Throughout the Bible there are scriptures on love. Many depict the depth of God's love for us. Others describe the love we should show others. What you may have missed is that loving others includes loving yourself – you are an "other"!

Why would I love myself? I didn't feel worthy of love from others. I never felt good enough. I always felt there had to be something wrong with me because none of the kids my age had the same type of home situation I had. No matter how perfect I performed at home, my mother's condition did not improve. I kept a large part of my life a secret from everyone, including friends, which made me feel like an imposter. Love myself…yeah right.

Here's the reality I did not understand until recently. How do you truly know how to love others unless you have first mastered loving yourself? You don't know. The walls I built to protect my family's secret also kept me from developing close relationships with others and myself. A part of me was cut off from everyone. Loving myself meant I had to tear down this wall and expose the true Jannette to myself. It's not enough to be open and accepting of others. You must accept who you are, weaknesses and all. Loving yourself means to trust yourself and to treat yourself with respect, kindness and compassion.

This was so hard for me to wrap my mind around. I had to accept that accomplishments do not determine whether I am lovable or not. Who I am (a child of God) makes me worthy of love. This is a truth I must remind myself of daily. Brené Brown said it the best, "I didn't want my level of self-love to limit how much I can love my children or my husband." For this reason, I want to be "all in." I want to have enough courage to connect with the people around me. This is not possible unless you love completely, which includes loving yourself.

Loving yourself also applies to accepting how you look. I have never felt confident about my appearance. I viewed myself as the ugly duckling that never transformed into the beautiful swan. In my mind, I was always too fat, too pale, too plain looking, and the list goes on and on. And much like the negative behaviors I learned by watching my anxious mother, my negative thoughts were affecting how I represented myself to others. Basically, I hid as much of my physical self as I did my emotional self. Baggy clothes, not leaving the house without make-up, and constant dieting was my lifestyle.

God impressed on my heart that I needed to accept myself and present all of me to the world. My first thought was, "Ugh – why?" but I realized it wasn't fair for me to ask others to trust me enough to be their authentic selves if I was not willing to do the same. So, I read every scripture on love in the Bible and started applying what I learned to myself. I told myself "good job" if I accomplished a goal. I made a list of positive traits I possessed and read it whenever I started to feel unlovable. Every morning I told myself, "You are adorable" when I headed out for the day. Silly? Maybe, but the more I said these things out loud (to myself), the more I began to believe them. I can honestly say that I now love and even like myself. And because I love myself, I now understand how to love others as well.

Final Thoughts

I often wonder how I can change my perspective from years of being wired to survive and protect. Ezekiel 36: 26-27 provided the answer.

> Moreover, I will give you a new heart and put a new spirit within you, and I will remove the heart of stone from your

> flesh and give you a heart of flesh. I will put my Spirit within you and cause you to walk in My statutes, and you will keep My ordinances and do them.

That's the beauty of God's promises to us. I don't have to be rewired. I only have to ask God to fill me with His Spirit (the Holy Spirit), and healthy thoughts will abound in my mind. With God's help, the negative thoughts constantly playing over and over in my head were replaced with positive thoughts. And to remain strong, I follow the advice given in Philippians 4:8-9.

> Finally, brothers and sisters, whatever is true, whatever is noble, whatever is right, whatever is pure, whatever is lovely, whatever is admirable – if anything is excellent or praiseworthy – think about such things. Whatever you have learned or received or heard from me, or seen in me – put it into practice. And the God of peace will be with you.

My childhood does not define who I am, but it is a part of me. You do not have to "overcome" your past. The goal is to continue to work through it. Just remember to keep moving forward. The perfectionist in you will scream, "That's not good enough," but it is. You do not have to be perfect; you just have to show up. Hope and joy are not produced by being perfect. They come from being present and loving yourself. Yes, yourself.

I realize now that peace and joy are what I crave most for my life. Peace and joy come from having a hopeful attitude. So, like telling myself daily that I am adorable, I also tell myself I am enough. I am worthy of having connections and worthy of the love others give me. I do not have to perform perfectly to earn acceptance. I just have to be present. I am enough, and so are you.

JOYFUL BEGINNINGS

"May the God of hope fill you with all joy and peace as you trust in Him, so that you may overflow with hope by the power of the Holy Spirit."

– Romans 15:13

When I look back, I realize that I have lived most of my life on edge, never truly relaxing or enjoying the moment. Whether it was during my childhood, during college, the first year of marriage, or after I became a mother, there was always a sense of tension inside me. Worry and doubt surrounded every moment, and this seemed normal to me. I now realize that is not a healthy way to approach life. It may have been necessary as a child raised in a family with mental illness, but it does not have to continue.

In the past, I have lived a "half" life. I went through the motions, allowed others to define my success and stayed on alert for dreadful things to happen instead of expecting good things. It was exhausting. When I started this discovery process, more than anything, I wanted to feel as though I was living my life to its fullness. I wanted to experience joy throughout each day, followed by peace in any circumstance. However, I had no idea how to achieve that state of being.

Joy and peace are what I crave most in my life. What exactly is joy? It's more than being happy. Happiness is an emotion that you experience. It comes and goes with a situation. Joy resides in your spirit, and it is a way of being. Joy doesn't rely on circumstances, but it is developed within a person. It really is a way of living your life.

How do you live a life of joy? Great question. To a certain degree, that differs for every person, but I have discovered that it is a choice. You can choose to protect yourself from painful situations by building emotional barriers that others cannot penetrate. But by doing this, you also prevent joy from penetrating those walls. Joy is a decision to have a positive outlook despite your surroundings. Joy is believing in yourself and thinking the best of others. Joy is living in love.

For most of my life, I never allowed myself to relax. I enjoyed moments such as family gatherings, vacations or time spent playing with my sons. However, once the event was over, I focused on preparing for the next trial ahead of me. This type of living doesn't leave room for continuous joy. It focuses on the possibility of negative situations instead of choosing to be content in the now.

Needless to say, always preparing for the next issue to arise is tiring. In my search for joy, I realized that I needed to place my trust in God and not in myself. For me to break a lifetime of anticipating the worst required a major shift. When I began to focus on God's will for my life, instead of anticipating the next crisis, guess what I found? Joy. Unexplainable happiness that has changed my perspective.

Hopefully you won't need a major life change like I did. Choose joy as a lifestyle now. This requires putting your trust in God to fight your battles instead of relying on your own abilities. Joy is obtainable when you decide to do the following:

1. Let go – instead of constantly trying to figure things out in your life, allow God to direct you on the appropriate action to take. Following God's direction daily leads you to joy. You are not alone; God is always with you. Trust Him to provide whatever strength is needed at the appropriate time. By doing this, you will become free to focus on loving others and being a positive influence, instead of dreading the next problem that arises. It is true, there will always be problems in life, but how we face those problems dictates whether we allow ourselves to live a joyful life.

2. Stop the negativity – Refuse to allow negative thoughts to run through your mind. Replace them with positive thoughts. If you allow yourself to constantly relive your past mistakes in your thoughts, you will remain defeated. If, however, you focus your thoughts on your strengths, on the positive things or people in your life, and on God's

promises, your focus will remain positive. Joyce Meyer says, "You can be pitiful or powerful, not both." The battle begins with what you spend your time thinking. Draw strength by focusing on power thoughts, not on a personal pity party.

3. Be flexible – Life is everchanging which should create excitement, not dread. If you are stiff and rigid in the way you approach your life, you will never find peace. Relinquishing control to God, instead of relying on your own abilities, is critical to having a joyful life. For child caregivers, this is extraordinarily difficult because of the responsibilities we were given at an early age. Hopefully, you now see that trying to remain in control of every situation is not healthy, nor is it God's plan for your life. God will guide you through new and difficult situations. He provides the strength and agility needed to make it through any challenge successfully.

4. Be thankful – This is a HUGE part of finding joy and peace. Until you stop to genuinely appreciate what you have been given, you will never find joy. The key here is to STOP and appreciate. Life is flowing past us at record speeds. There always seems to be another issue to address, another need to be met. It's easy to forget to appreciate the things around us as we speed off to the next item on our to-do list. Carefully consider what you are thankful for

in your life. Make it a point to thank other people for their kindness. Thank God daily for all that He has provided to you. And remember to state your thankfulness, not just think it. Words spoken release a power that you can use to promote a joyful life.

Eye of the Storm

Scripture reveals that faith, hope, and most importantly love are all needed to maintain joy. The four actions described earlier help to create an environment that will support all three in your life. But how do you develop faith? How do you develop hope? Through my research, I discovered that having faith breeds hope and having hope feeds joy. But where is love in all of this? I had all the ingredients for joy. I just didn't know how to combine them for the desired result. That's when I thought of a tornado.

I grew up in the area meteorologists call Tornado Alley because of the number of tornadoes that hit this part of the country. Safety is extremely important during these events. If I am being honest, however, I tend to look outside to catch a glimpse of the tornado before taking cover. I have been extremely fortunate not to have been caught in a tornado as it touched down. There have been a few tornadoes that have passed over my house without inflicting damage. It's amazing to watch. In the beginning, you are surrounded by a strong thunderstorm with heavy rains and often hail. Then all of a sudden, the winds calm down, the rain and hail stop, and it seems – for a moment – that the storm is over. That's when the wind starts again, and the rain and hail pour down as if it had never stopped. This surreal calm within the storm is referred to as the eye of the tornado.

In simple terms, a tornado can occur within a thunderstorm if warm, humid air rises as the cool air containing rain and sometimes hail falls. This combination causes the air currents to spin inside the thunderstorm. If the spinning winds gain enough strength, the tail or end of the tunnel created can touch the ground, producing a tornado. Tornadoes are strong enough to move massive objects easily. So, imagine faith is the warm, humid air and hope is the cool air. This mixture creates a spinning air current that grows in strength as love is introduced into the mix. And just like a tornado, at the eye of this love storm is joy and peace (calmness). Faith, hope and love all work together in your life to create joy and peace. Like a tornado, when the three work together, obstacles such as fear, doubt and negativity are moved out of the way so that joy and peace can be discovered.

Faith

What exactly is faith? Faith is placing your trust in God. This type of trust is given freely, not earned. In other words, God doesn't have to provide for us or show us how He will accomplish what we ask. In our hearts, we have faith – an understanding that God will provide, in His own timing, whatever we need to accomplish His plan. This way of believing is opposite of how the world operates. "I'll believe it when I see it," is the view of the world. Trust is hard to find in the world, but it is not uncommon with God.

Without faith, joy can be taken away by thoughts of impending doom, also known as evil forebodings. I spent many years allowing this false sense of doom to steal my joy. I thought I was gifted with a "sixth" sense that allowed me to feel when terrible things were about to happen. It may sound silly, but the feelings were real.

I treated these feelings as Spidey senses like Spiderman uses to detect danger. However, what I didn't realize was the danger I was detecting happened in the past; it was not a warning for the future. Years of trying to be prepared for any problem faced by my family during my childhood, created these outbursts of anxious feelings that would sporadically arise as an adult. Now I know that to defeat these negative feelings only requires a positive attitude. So, when anxiety hits, and I start to worry about anything and everything, I fight back with positive thoughts. I think about all the things I am thankful for in my life. I think about the good things I have experienced recently. Most importantly, I think about the promises written in God's word, such as the promise of comfort and hope declared in Isaiah.

> *"Do not fear, for I have redeemed you [from captivity]; I have called you by name; you are Mine!"*
> *– Isaiah 43:1*

The word "redeemed" jumped out as I read this scripture. God has released me from the captivity of my youth. As a child, I felt responsible for not only caring for my mother but also her happiness. The fear of failure held me captive. Now, I understand that I am not responsible for the success or happiness of others. My responsibility is to follow God's direction. According to God, I am worthy; I am enough.

> Trust in *and* rely confidently on the Lord with all your heart and do not rely on your own insight *or* understanding. In all your ways know *and* acknowledge *and* recognize Him, and He will make your paths straight *and* smooth [removing obstacles that block your way].
> – Proverbs 3:5-6

Not being able to control the future or know what it holds is difficult. This scripture reveals that we must rely on God to guide our direction. He knows the outcome and which paths lead to success. If we quiet our mind (stop trying to figure things out on our own understanding) and listen for God's direction, joy will follow.

I have always put my trust in God, but I haven't always relied on Him. That's tricky for a caregiver. You have been the person your family relies on. To turn over that control, even to God, is scary. This scripture reminds us to not rely on the plans we make or the emotions we feel but to confidently rely on God to direct our actions.

Trust

The practical, day-to-day side of faith incorporates trusting others. If we trust God to take care of us, then we must also believe He will not allow others to harm us. Why then, should we not trust others, unless God tells us different?

I always believed I was a trusting person. However, in retrospect, trusting people and accepting people are two different things. To trust requires each party to be vulnerable with one another. To accept others requires compassion. I had plenty of compassion, but the thought of being vulnerable, as discussed earlier, frightened me.

As an adult, it became increasingly difficult to trust others and develop close relationships. There was a part of me that on a subconscious level felt like a fraud. How do I explain my childhood to people who have never experienced mental illness in their families? I have a mentally ill parent who's not crazy, just anxious. What would they think?

During conversations, other people would reminisce about their childhoods. Stories of family trips or going away to camps always surfaced. When asked about my favorite childhood memories, I would quickly turn the conversation back to their experiences. Who wanted to hear that my best childhood experiences involved staying home with my mother, watching General Hospital and buying groceries with my dad? There was always a part of me that I had to hide, and this made me feel like a fraud, just waiting for someone to realize that I was inadequate. In essence, I never felt safe to be myself. If I'm honest, I never felt safe at all.

I still struggle with security. It's not that I feel I live in an unsafe world – I just feel there is an underlying current which suggests that safety doesn't truly exist. As I mentioned earlier, a therapist told me to visualize my safe place whenever my emotions felt uncontrollable. This would help center my mind and allow me to feel the emotions without being overwhelmed. There was just one problem. I couldn't imagine a safe place. I couldn't imagine feeling safe anywhere or in any situation.

In today's world, everyone seeks a safe haven. Even though I don't have it here on earth, I do have a safe haven through God. Instead of focusing on a place, I focus on God's will and teachings that state God is my shelter, always. My safety comes from God. He's my safe place. Psalm 91:1 reads, "He who dwells in the shelter of the Most High will remain secure and rest in the shadow of the Almighty."

As a child, I had no problem believing the Bible stories about Daniel in the lion's den or David defeating Goliath. A man spending the night with lions and surviving because God protected him seemed plausible. A boy defeating a giant with a slingshot could absolutely happen. However, as I entered adulthood, believing in the simple explanations became harder and harder. There has to be a twist, right? Someone must be manipulating the story to get an advantage over someone else.

Somewhere along the way, our adult vision becomes jaded with fear and distrust. As a child, all things seemed possible. However, after living in a world that doesn't always exude compassion, love or even joy, possibilities become tainted with abuse, deception and fear. I don't want to live that way. I realize now, that it is a choice. I can choose to allow the negativity of the world shape how I view my surroundings, or I can choose to follow Biblical principles and allow God's love to shape my view. This requires trust of others and trust in God.

Hope

As a child, I felt I had to prepare for the worst-case scenario to protect my mother and myself. My family often referred to bad experiences as the "Hutson Luck." It seemed liked every time we were experiencing good times, something would arise to throw a kink in our plans. My family expected it to happen and even tried to plan for the arrival of the Hutson Luck.

In essence, I had more confidence in bad things happening to me than good things. That is the opposite of having hope. To let go of expecting dreadful things to happen (and planning for the unexpected) is hard. That was my safety net. When you are raised in an environment in which you never know whether it will be a good day or bad day, you must be prepared for the bad day in order to survive.

According to the Merriam-Webster dictionary, hope is to confidently expect something to happen. In the past, I used optimism and hope interchangeably. Optimism is to anticipate the best possible outcome. When faced with a challenge, I generally anticipate a positive result, but I am prepared for it to not happen. In other words, I didn't *confidently* expect a positive result happening for me.

However, that is not the same as hope. Hope is having faith that good will overcome evil regardless of the situation. Hope is knowing that everything will work out to benefit all parties involved. I struggle with hope. My childhood trained me to have a plan A, plan B, and if I'm honest, a plan C. The first plan will most likely fail so plan B and C are designed to be the safety net.

This way of thinking robs you from true joy. Hope is required to enjoy each day, and hope requires that you honestly believe good things are going to happen for you. That left me with the question of how to rewire my thoughts to be hopeful.

I started by making a list of every Bible scripture related to hope and studied each one to determine how I could apply the principle of each to my daily life. The first one on my list was Psalm 33:18. This scripture explains that those who fear God and follow His will can confidently hope for good things to happen through God's compassion and care. There's that confident word again. To apply this principle, God becomes your safety net instead of your plan B, C, D, etc. To have hope, you must rely on God, not yourself. In other words, your confidence must come from God, not from what you produce or do.

You have to purposely believe good things are going to happen. It's a choice. Actions we take should represent our hope in practice. To activate hope in your life requires the following four actions:

1. You must rejoice and look forward to good things happening;
2. You must believe good things will happen even in difficult times;
3. You must be patient as you wait for good things to happen; and,
4. You must continually pray for guidance.

Hope does not require a safety net. I encourage you to find scriptures of your own that guide and build your faith so that you can turn hopeless planning (such as always having backup plans just in case) into hope filled actions that will guide your life to a healthy path full of joy.

Love

We discussed the importance of loving yourself, as well as others in the "You Are Enough" chapter. Without accepting and taking care of yourself, you cannot love others. Loving one another is the reason we exist. Without love, our actions are meaningless.

But how do you truly express love to another person? It's not in our acts, but rather it's in the motives that surround our acts. To show love, in the biblical sense, requires that we do not get offended easily with one another. It demands honesty and justice. It removes all aspects of pride and places the focus on others. Love protects, believes the best in others, hopes for positive outcomes, and lasts forever.

This type of love, which fosters joy and peace, comes from God, not the world. As you strengthen your faith and develop a hopeful attitude, love grows within you and develops that peaceful center for your life. As I Corinthians 13:13 reminds us, "And now these three remain: faith, hope and love. But the greatest of these is love."

Joy Begins Now

The world today does not promote joy. It promotes self-sufficiency, love of material things and finding fault in others. To have joy means to value biblical principles instead of the values established by the world. Remember, God never changes. Do not allow the world and its demands to get in the way of your relationship with God. He will direct you to the path that leads to a joyful life.

BOUNDARIES

"Now the Lord is the Spirit, and where the Spirit of the Lord is, there is freedom."
– 2 Corinthians 3:17

Remember the term "false sense of responsibility" from the "People Pleaser" section of the "You Are Enough" chapter? It's when a person takes responsibility for things that are outside their scope of control. There are several reasons why someone may take on this extra burden. It may be due to guilt associated with the situation. It could be the result of pride if a person believes they are the only one who can fix the problem. It can also be associated with people-pleasing. You accept the responsibility because others expect you to take care of issues for them. Child-caregivers are especially prone to this false sense of responsibility when they are tasked with caring for a parent. As a child, it is difficult to understand where your responsibility ends, so you assume responsibility for everything.

It is obvious that this is an impossible task. People with the tendency to assume responsibility for all things set themselves up for failure. How can you be all things to all people? You can't. So, expectations are not met. This leaves you feeling like a failure, when in reality, the issue at hand was not yours to manage.

This feeling of being responsible for everyone's success, everyone's happiness followed me into adulthood. When I say everyone, I mean everyone. I felt responsible for my boss at work being successful. I felt responsible for my husband's happiness, even if he didn't ask for my help. I felt responsible for my children being accepted and successful at school. I even felt responsible for the safety of other drivers on the road around me. I once followed an elderly person on the highway several miles so that other cars wouldn't get too close to their bumper. And of course, I felt responsible for my mother's happiness. That never left me.

In my mind, part of helping other people meant I should take on part of the responsibility for their success. If I didn't help them, who would? The balanced person would say they can help themselves! I was not balanced. My childhood placed additional responsibilities on me that I never questioned; that assumed responsibility grew as I became older, and it synced well with my people-pleasing tendencies.

The reality is it is not healthy for you or the person you are "helping" if you assume responsibility for their well-being. It's not achievable. And to be blunt, you are not all that. A person's happiness is their responsibility – no one else's. Being helpful means to provide assistance to people when asked, not planning a 3-step process that leads them to where you believe they will be happy. It's not your responsibility. The best help you can provide someone is the space to find their own way.

So, how do you recognize this false sense of responsibility? How do you release yourself from this unhealthy behavior? This false sense of responsibility is sometimes referred to as toxic guilt. Toxic guilt occurs when we feel guilty, even if we didn't do anything wrong. It often grows from feeling responsible for others' health or happiness. Can you say child caregiver? That is the theme of my entire childhood. My mother's health and happiness were always at the core of my family's decisions. Unfortunately, I carried that into other relationships outside of my family. I thought it was normal to put others' happiness before my own. If others I helped were successful, then I was successful. That's lovely, but many people will take advantage of that personality trait. Many. It is not necessary to disregard your happiness to help others. It should go hand in hand.

This was another area I struggled with understanding and accepting. I always valued my ability to help others. In reality, I wasn't helping, I was controlling. I was taking all the responsibility off the person – whether they wanted me to or not – and charging forward with what I thought would be best. I know this is difficult to believe, but I don't actually know what's best for everyone. If I'm honest with myself, my taking on responsibility for others usually ended in me feeling like a failure because whatever action I took didn't resolve the issue at hand. I felt guilty for not being able to make everyone happy.

Once I realized I was not responsible for the happiness of others, it felt like a load of bricks was lifted off of me. If God directs me to help someone and I complete that task, I've met my obligation. The rest remains the responsibility of the person I helped. In my mother's situation, if my brothers and I help her find a safe place to live and obtain medical care as needed, our obligation has been met. Her happiness lies with her and the decisions she makes for herself. I am not responsible for my mother's happiness. I can't explain how freeing that realization was for me. I felt like a whole section in my heart became available allowing me to consider what makes me happy. What do I want for my life? I can be first in line for my own help. It's an amazing feeling!

The next time you feel stress that a situation is not working out as planned, take a moment and ask yourself if the situation is truly your responsibility. Does it affect your livelihood, your health or your happiness? If not, take a step back and allow the affected person to take the lead. Life brings enough challenges for you to manage. Taking on others' responsibilities is too much. Being there as a friend or offering resources are both wonderful ways to show support. But if you start feeling guilty for the situation or guilty if what you offer doesn't resolve the issue for the other person, you've crossed into toxic guilt. As a caregiver, your family member's life came first. That is not healthy for you or your family member. Your health must come first. You will not be helpful to anyone if you are not healthy, both physically and mentally.

Responsibilities

Discerning which responsibilities are yours to manage can be difficult for former child caregivers. Our people-pleasing desire can rationalize the need to take on everyone's problems. The reality is that what we take on to manage should be directed by God. In the Bible, there are several scriptures that describe what responsibilities God places in our lives. 1 Thessalonians 5:12-22 provides clear instructions on what we are urged to do in our daily lives. It reveals we are responsible for the following action items:

1. Appreciate the leaders that have authority over you. I believe leaders referenced here include not only governmental leaders but leaders in your workplace, teachers, church leaders and elders of your family. To extend appreciation means to show them love, respect, and peaceful interactions. It does not mean to do their work and take responsibility if they are not successful.
2. Hold others accountable. If you witness someone taking advantage of others or continually making bad decisions, it is important to help guide them to the correct path. This

may be in the form of a direct conversation presented in a kind, loving manner – not in an in-your-face manner. It can also be as simple as being the example of how to behave correctly for this person to follow.

3. Encourage other people who lack confidence. Help others recognize their value and what gifts they offer. This also applies to yourself – you should be your own biggest fan.

4. Help those that are weak find strength. This is a caregiver's specialty. However, doing things for weak individuals and helping those that are weak are two different things. There is a fine line between supporting someone by encouraging them as they learn how to handle their own responsibilities and transferring ownership of those responsibilities to yourself.

5. Be patient with others, including yourself. This is extremely hard for perfectionists. Many times, it is easier to do a task yourself than to watch someone stumble through the process. Being patient requires allowing others the time needed to learn how to manage tasks on their own. It also means being patient with yourself as you learn new things. Making mistakes is part of the learning process.

6. Do what is best for others. In other words, if someone wrongs you, do not "pay them back" with the same treatment. This may be hard, but do what's right even if

the other person did not extend you the same courtesy. You can't control another person's actions, but you can control your own. Be the example for others to follow.

7. Rejoice and delight in your faith. God is amazing and provides everything we need to lead joyous lives. Remember this daily.

8. Pray continually. Open, ongoing communication with God helps keep your perspective healthy and provides the strength you need. You are never alone; He is always available to listen and help.

9. Be thankful and give thanks continually in all circumstances. One thing joyful people have in common is that they have a thankful nature. Joy and thanksgiving go hand in hand.

10. Accept the guidance of the Holy Spirit. Do you ever get a feeling in your gut that something is not right, or you should take a specific action at a specific time? This is often referred to as intuition. Actually, this is a gift from God – the Holy Spirit. The Spirit helps you determine what is good and what is evil. It helps guide you, if you listen, to the best decision or course of action. Listen to that small voice – it's one of the many ways God provides guidance to you.

These instructions strongly urge people to help one another, be examples for each other, and follow the guidance provided by God. It does not include taking responsibility for the success, failure or happiness of others. This may seem strange, but this was hard for me to understand. To support or help my mother required me to take actions and own the results. I now understand this was not healthy for me or my mother. There must be boundaries established that define what I am responsible for managing and what belongs to my mother.

Healthy Boundaries

Boundaries set the limits on what a person can expect you to do for them. These limits may be related to emotional support, actual work performed for a person or how often you will be in contact with a person. Boundaries are necessary to create an invisible line that separates you from the needs of another person, while providing space to allow you to feel safe and respected. Boundaries may be created as a physical, mental or emotional barrier – whatever is needed in a relationship. We all have specific comfort zones in any given situation. Boundaries help keep your comfort level in the healthy range.

So, what are the benefits of establishing healthy boundaries? Defining boundaries helps you communicate your comfort level to others. It helps identify when and how to say no to a request made of you. It helps others set realistic expectations on how you can help or support them in times of need. And most importantly, a healthy boundary is designed to ensure your needs are considered first. That is critical for child caregivers who were raised in an environment that always put other family members' needs first.

    My mother was accustomed to asking me for whatever she believed she needed, and I would comply. Often this meant putting my family's needs or my own aside while I met her need. This routinely occurred until my father passed away. My brothers helped me establish healthy boundaries with my mother by offering their assistance. They knew I couldn't handle the guilt of not meeting my mother's expectations. So, they told me whenever Mom asked me to do something to tell her that I wasn't available to help and encourage her to call one of them for assistance. That gave me the distance I needed to overcome my people-pleasing tendencies – or in this case, my mother-pleasing tendencies – and work towards having a relationship built on healthier behaviors with my mother. Eventually, Mom went straight to the boys for her needs. My brothers were strong enough to distinguish when my mother truly needed assistance and when she could handle things on her own. This discernment not only helped me create healthy boundaries for my relationship with my mother, but it also strengthened my mother's ability to care for herself.

Boundaries provide personal space to feel safe. When my father passed away, my mother expected me to do all the things he managed for her. Any time I was around her I felt anxious and trapped. I was raised to do as she asked, but it was not possible to live my life and manage my mother's life as well. As adults, child caregivers have to establish these boundaries to set family members' expectations appropriately. My mother was not trying to take advantage of me. She was responding to how our family dynamic had been arranged. If my father wasn't available, I filled in. She was alone, scared and resorted to what she knew. It was my responsibility as an adult, to establish healthy expectations and healthy boundaries for our relationship. And it was hard, really hard. Luckily, my brothers supported me and provided the wisdom needed to determine which needs were true needs my mother needed assistance with versus those needs she should be handling herself. Setting boundaries is so important for your well-being and to break the anxiety cycle. Even if you have to do it alone, do it. Setting boundaries will increase your ability to be compassionate and care for your loved one, as well as yourself.

Guidance

How do you know whether it's necessary to establish a boundary? If the relationship consists of an unhealthy balance, such as one person puts more into the relationship than the other, then boundaries are needed. For child caregivers, this is almost always the case. And as we develop relationships as adults, it is easy to transfer this formula to others outside our family. I know I did. I didn't ask for help or encouragement from others, I supplied it to them. I thought that was how relationships worked. Unfortunately, during a difficult period in my life, there was no one available to help me through it. They didn't know how to help because I had never opened up and allowed them to do so. In fact, my friends continued to come to me for assistance while I was facing difficulties in my life. I felt alone, even though I was surrounded by friends. That's not healthy either.

Think about a close relationship you have with a friend or family member, and ask yourself the following questions:

- Do you constantly feel taken advantage of by this person?
- Are you agreeing to do things to keep them happy, even if it creates difficulties for you?
- Do you avoid conflict with this person by saying yes to whatever is asked of you?
- Do you accept whatever level of friendship is offered because you fear being rejected?
- Do you do whatever is necessary to maintain this relationship because you want to be accepted or receive approval from this person?

If you answered yes to any of these questions, the relationship is most likely not balanced. Creating a healthy boundary will reset the relationship so that both individuals benefit. You do not have to be the martyr for others. Your well-being is just as important.

You should always consider your personal values when creating a boundary. What is important to you? I was raised that children respect and care for their parents. That's one of my personal values. When I established a healthy boundary with my mom, it allowed me to provide care for my mother while taking care of myself. It's the invisible line between providing the care my mom needs from me (not desires) and providing the space I need to feel safe and respected. I do not allow myself to cross this boundary. In the beginning, my mom wasn't really happy with me saying no, but she survived. She also started taking care of things on her own which increased her self-confidence. I discovered the boundary helped not only me, but my mother as well.

The boundaries you establish for your relationships will be unique to you. Only you know what is needed to keep you feeling safe and respected, and it will be different for every relationship you have with others. Some boundaries will be flexible because you have established more trust with the other person, and this allows you to feel safe even if the boundary changes periodically. Other relationships will require a stiffer boundary that doesn't change often. That's what I needed for my relationship with my mother. This was unfamiliar territory for both of us. Having the boundary helped me to respect my mother while taking care of myself.

Boundaries also protect you from taking on that false sense of responsibility we discussed earlier. The more responsibilities you own, the more energy you burn trying to meet those needs. That leaves little time or energy for showing empathy towards others. Empathy is powerful. Showing another person that you understand how they feel and that you have faced similar situations often provides the hope they need to overcome their struggles. If you just fix the problem for them, they never gain the self-confidence created by overcoming a problem. Taking on responsibilities for other people may appear on the surface to help them, but in reality, it only makes them more reliant on you instead of themselves. Boundaries help you be the encourager, not the enabler. Being present for them is enough.

Needs Versus Rights

Growing up, my focus was on the needs of others. Due to my mother's mental illness, she had needs specific to her care. My father needed assistance with household chores, like grocery shopping. As a parent, I focused on the needs of my children. The only needs I didn't focus on were my own. I had them. I communicated them, but at the end of the day, I always put the needs of others before my own. That's how you care for others –

right? Not necessarily. To help others, you must take care of yourself first. If you constantly push your needs aside, you become like a martyr. Once we take this position, it is easy to become prideful in our actions instead of helping others out of love.

By taking care of ourselves, we approach helping others from a healthy state. Before you begin to address the needs of others, you need to make sure your rights have been recognized. Rights? Yes, you have the right to be healthy and to take care of yourself first. For example, you have the right to tell someone you are not available to help without feeling guilty or having an excuse. You have the right to be treated with respect. Your needs are just as important as your family members or friends. You have the right to make mistakes and a right to be forgiven by others and yourself. No one can take these rights away from you without your permission. Don't allow it. Your health matters too.

Practice, Practice, Practice

Establishing a boundary will most likely feel foreign at first. It did for me. Practice, however, makes perfect. Force yourself to communicate the boundary to your loved one and enforce it. You may have to distance yourself more than normal if you receive push back from the other person. This is common and is not a reflection on you. Change is hard for anyone. My mom didn't like it when I told her I couldn't handle something for her, but she could do it. That wasn't the response she was looking for or used to getting from me. However, over time, she accepted the boundaries I established, and it wasn't an issue. I gained a sense of control that I didn't have previously. Instead of feeling trapped and anxious when I was around my mother, I started to feel calm and confident. I still have bouts of anxiety, but I rely on my boundary to guide me when making decisions that relate to my mother. The boundaries I established and maintain allow my mother and I to have a healthy relationship with one another.

 Boundaries are hard for child caregivers to establish with family members struggling with mental illness. I know. But you have to remember, your mental health is just as important as your family member's. I am not responsible for my mother's illness. You are not responsible for your family member's illness. You need to grasp this truth. If you continue to take on the responsibilities of others, you will burn out and have nothing left to care for anyone, including yourself. So, what is keeping you from building healthy boundaries and detaching yourself from the responsibilities that belong to other people? Is it the false sense of responsibility for others? Is it guilt or shame related to your childhood? Is it your need to please people? Whatever the reason, do not ignore these feelings. Work through your fear and protect your health. Maybe you need to journal to get those bottled-up fears out of your system. Or perhaps, daily prayer time, Bible study, professional counselling, or talking with a close friend can provide the sounding board needed to work through these emotions. Whatever works for you, do it. Just like the emotions we bottled up inside of us to maintain that calm environment in our childhood, these emotions will build up and manifest into emotional and physical ailments. Boundaries provide a way to turn these unhealthy behaviors into healthy actions. Boundaries empower you to help others while maintaining your own health.

Fruits of the Spirit

Earlier we discussed the true responsibilities we each have, according to Christian beliefs. These responsibilities included following the guidance of the Holy Spirit. The Holy Spirit is a gift from God that helps us to discern right from wrong. It's the feeling you get in the pit of your stomach when something doesn't seem right. It's that small voice inside your head that tries to steer you in the right direction. The more you quiet your thoughts, the more you will hear the Spirit's direction. And this direction is available to you 24/7.

> *"And the Spirit of the Lord shall rest upon him, the Spirit of wisdom and understanding, the Spirit of counsel and might, the Spirit of knowledge and the fear of the Lord."*
> *– Isaiah 11:2*

If we follow the guidance provided by the Spirit, scripture tells us that we will be given the "fruit" of the Spirit. This means, by listening to God's guide and basing our actions on His guidance, we will develop love for others and ourselves, joy, inner peace, patience, kindness, goodness, faithfulness, gentleness and self-control. Why is this important? Without these "fruits," we cannot fully use the gifts God has given us. Allowing the Spirit to guide our actions using the fruits described above actually empowers our gifts. The two combined provide the best results. As you demonstrate the fruits of the Spirit, you gain strength and confidence. This strength enables you to help others. It's like exercise for your soul!

The Spirit's guidance can also be used to establish the appropriate boundaries in relationships. Ask God to provide this guidance to you. What areas of your relationship makes you feel uncomfortable? What actions are expected of you that make you feel anxious? How do you remove yourself from these situations without harming the other person? I found by praying for the Spirit to guide me, I was able to see through my emotions and find healthy ways to manage the relationship with boundaries. God will provide the direction you need. If you follow it, you will begin finding that the fruits listed above (joy, peace, faithfulness, etc.) bloom in your everyday life.

BELIEVE

"May the God of hope fill you with all joy and peace in believing [through the experience of your faith] that by the power of the Holy Spirit you will abound in hope and overflow with confidence in His promises."
– Romans 15:13

As I worked through the emotions and strongholds from my youth, it became apparent to me that I had something blocking me from completely trusting God. I had no problem with trusting God to help me help others, but when it came to God helping me, at times, my trust waned. Particularly, if the challenge I faced had to do with anxiety, I did not believe God would help me for the sake of me. I trusted God to enable me to help others but not to help myself.

The challenge for me was twofold. First, as a child I buried the disappointment I felt towards God for not delivering me from the bondage created by my mother's illness. I hid these feelings because I thought it was a sin to be mad at God, and I was afraid I would lose His love if I allowed myself to express the disappointment I felt. This was one of the last emotions that surfaced while facing the impact of my youth, and it was the most difficult to face.

My second challenge was admitting I was angry at God for allowing anxiety to affect me as an adult. The Word teaches that you do not have to earn God's love. It is given freely to those who love and obey Him. Why then, did He not deliver me from the anxiety? Why must I struggle with anxiety when I spent my life taking care of my mom? If I didn't do anything wrong, and the Word says He loves regardless, why would He allow me to suffer?

Inner Child Tantrum

Buried deep inside me was disappointment and anger towards God. These feelings had existed since my childhood. Trying to process an emotion that is buried inside since childhood is hard. The feeling was captured through a child's perspective. How do you process a child's anger and disappointment as an adult? My lack of trust that God would help me through my own battles with anxiety created a weakness in my faith. I needed to address it. Anxiety had a way of showing up just in time to create a barrier that kept me from enjoying my life. For example, driving became a literal roadblock for me.

As I mentioned in an earlier chapter, my mother inadvertently taught me to be anxious while driving, especially in high traffic situations. For many years, I avoided driving on major highways, especially for long distances. When I say avoid, I really mean I never did it. I thought my anxiety towards driving stemmed from me having a panic attack while driving at night on a major highway. I was afraid it would happen again. I now understand it was just an area that my anxiety decided to surface. Instead of facing my fear, I found workarounds by finding routes utilizing back roads or side streets. I would tag along with others going to the same destination. I avoided highways at all costs.

When I finally decided to face this fear, I realized my avoidance strategy was the same one my mother used to handle her anxiety. As a child, it was my responsibility to help my mother avoid situations that caused anxiety. So, choosing to avoid driving made complete sense to Young Jannette, my inner child. The heightened physical responses I experienced when trying to face a fear, in this case driving, was Young Jannette's way of warning me not to do it. Her perspective was one of a powerless child. A child that had a limited view of the world. For me to successfully face fears, I had to assure Young Jannette that, as an adult, I had the ability to handle the situation. I had to model the successful behavior of facing anxiety that my mother was not able to model for me as a child. Anxiety was never addressed by adults in my childhood. Instead, situations were avoided to ensure anxiety was kept at bay. In Young Jannette's world, uncontrolled anxiety resulted in catastrophic events.

Whether it was anxiety due to my fear of driving, or any other fear I faced, the only way I was able to overcome anxious feelings was by doing it afraid and leaning on God. This meant that I had to believe that was God's plan for me all along.

I think about the struggle I faced with my fear of driving and realize now that God's plan involved more than me overcoming my anxiety while on a highway. It was so much more. Instead of delivering me from my fear, which is what I REALLY wanted and prayed for, He showed me weaknesses that were hampering my faith and holding me back. My fear wasn't due to a specific event associated with driving. It was due to a stronghold placed in my mind during childhood that manifested in doubt – doubt that God would help me overcome anxiety, whether it was the challenges created by my mother's anxiety or my own.

The doubt stemmed from watching my mother throughout my childhood battle episodes of debilitating anxiety. God saw her through the episodes, but He never delivered her completely from the illness. My mother was faithful to God in every respect. She read her Bible every morning and set aside prayer time in the morning and at night. Any direction she gave me and my brothers was based solidly on Biblical teachings and truths. In all aspects, she was a faithful servant. If God didn't deliver her then why would He deliver me? It had to be His will for my mom to remain this way, which I later translated to it was His will for me to stay burdened with anxiety. Paul had his "thorn" in his flesh (see 2 Corinthians 12); anxiety was my thorn, and I held onto this belief for the majority of my life.

After my father passed, God started preparing me to share my story to help others, which requires travel. Travel that I could not do because of my anxiety – anxiety that He refused to deliver me from (or so I thought). In my mind, God wanted me to do something He wouldn't equip me to do. As you can imagine, this made me angry – anger which I once again buried inside because I didn't want to be disrespectful to God. I felt like I had hit a brick wall – no, more like a brick maze with all the exits closed off.

To truly be free, I had to overcome the disappointment from my childhood and the anger I had against God as an adult. The first step was to recognize it existed. The next step was to pray for wisdom on how to replace the doubt and fear with positive emotions based on God's Word. This required more from me than driving down the highway calmly.

Anger, Deal With It

How do you forgive? Perhaps you need to forgive a parent, relative, sibling or friend for things that happened during your childhood. Or maybe you are like me, and you need to forgive God. To forgive is to cease to feel resentment against someone, or in this case, God. It's a voluntary transformation of your feelings and behavior toward an individual (or God) so you no longer feel resentment. Notice both explanations of forgiveness contain "feelings." As we have discussed, feelings need to be acknowledged, processed and recognized for what they are...emotions.

To forgive God, you have to be honest with Him about how you feel. He already knows so it won't be a shocker to Him. I wrote my feelings down to help process why I was angry. As I discovered the source of my anger, God gave me the answer as to why He chose to act (or not act) in the manner He did. God may not always choose to explain His actions, but writing it down helped me to process my feelings and understand where they originated.

R.T. Kendall wrote a book entitled, *Totally Forgiving God: When It Seems He Has Betrayed You*. In the book, he discusses the "betrayal barrier," which is created when we feel betrayed by God. This weakness in our faith creates a barrier that prevents us from truly trusting God. In reality, God never betrays us, but because of the circumstances we face in life, we sometimes feel as though He did. The key word here is *feel*.

According to R.T. Kendall, to break the betrayal barrier you must first realize that God wants you to break the barrier between the two of you. Take this opportunity to get to know God by studying His word and praying. Remember to avoid complaining about your circumstances. Complaining opens the door for the devil to bombard you with lies. Gratitude will silence these lies. By addressing the behaviors God guides you to change, you will become stronger in faith, ultimately removing the betrayal barrier from your path.

It's the Holy Spirit that will lead you to break the barrier. It's not always an external situation improving. Forgiving God allows you to let go of the past feelings of bitterness and opens up space for joy to take its place. It frees you from the guilt, anxiety and fear that has been pent up inside, creating holes in your faith.

After you admit how you truly feel to God, you need to make a list of all the blessings God has extended to you. And I mean all the blessings during your lifetime. As you reflect back in time, I believe you will be amazed at how many times God has been there for you – especially in the small day to day things.

Forgiveness is a choice. The feelings may surface again, but when they do, choose to forgive and let go of the anger, whether you feel like it or not. God never left me. I know that now. My doubt did not offend God because He knows my heart. God loves me and always has and always will. He loves you too.

Lessons Learned

What I learned from this experience is that God chooses not to deliver us from certain situations so that we can grow stronger spiritually. I also learned that I was viewing anxiety through my childhood lens and needed to refocus my view using what I know as an adult. God is trustworthy, He loves us, and He will always be there for us. Always. As for the anger, anger in and of itself, is not a sin. It is an emotion. It is an emotion that needs to be felt and processed. If left buried, anger will tear holes in our faith. These holes can be repaired by surrounding yourself with God's Word. However, if left unattended, the holes can be accessed by the devil to create doubt, fear, and anxious thoughts in an attempt to stop us from using our God-given gifts to help others.

Romans 8:18 states, "For I consider that the suffering of this present time are not worthy to be compared with the glory that is to be revealed to us." If we are patient, God will reveal His plan to us. Unfortunately, this usually is an "after the fact" realization. However, it is all the sweeter when we know our journey had a purpose, and we were confident enough in our faith to persevere.

In Hebrews, there are many stories of people that did not receive what they asked of God because He had something better planned for them. Even though they did not receive what they wanted, they continued forward because they had faith that God loved them and would take care of them. Doubt weakens the trust that faith is built upon. Without trust and faith in God, a joyous life is not attainable.

Overcoming the negative behaviors learned in our childhood, including struggles with anxiety, leads to freedom. Really, it is not the anxiety that is the issue. It is having complete faith in God that is being addressed. At the beginning of this process, the Holy Spirit placed a word in my heart that continues to resurface...*believe*. Believe there is a plan for your life. Believe that you are a gift from God. Believe that God loves you and wants the best for you. Believe!

Believe

Choose to believe God has a purpose for what happened and be patient while you wait to see His plan come to fruition. As a child, God prevented me from living a life of bitterness, and, He led me to view my role as being a blessing not a victim. This helped me to develop those positive traits we discussed earlier (empathy, compassion, resiliency, etc.).

God did deliver me from the bondage of my childhood. It was step by step that took forty-five years to complete, but He did it. Along the way, He gifted me the opportunity to be a blessing to others with compassion and encouragement. Two gifts that were developed while taking care of my mom and supporting my father.

To believe something will happen before you see any evidence is faith. God wants us to choose to believe in Him. Unfortunately, bitterness and fear often come in between our believing and create doubt on whether God will be there for us. Fortunately, God believes in us even when we don't believe in ourselves. 2 Corinthians 12:7-9 says God's grace is sufficient, His power is made perfect in weakness. God delays our breakthrough to get our attention. I wanted to conquer my fear of driving. God wanted me to wake up and realize anxiety was holding me back through many aspects of my life – not just in driving. He didn't resolve my driving issue quickly. He held it to gain my attention.

COMMUNITY BUILDING

"God has given each of you a gift from His great variety of spiritual gifts. Use them well to serve one another."
– I Peter 4:10

What comes to mind when you hear the word community? Maybe you envision the city you live in, your circle of friends, or even a church group. All of those are examples of a community. Community is about making connections with others, and the thought of connecting with others, as discussed earlier, has always made me anxious. So, it should be no surprise that I saved this topic for the end of the book!

Early on, I confused networking as building a community. Networking is when you establish relationships that are beneficial to you or the other person. These relationships may bring value in business transactions or personal initiatives. Many times, there is an implied, "You scratch my back, I'll scratch yours." To be honest, that didn't really sit well with me. I didn't want to base a relationship on what the other person could do for me. I wanted relationships with individuals that accepted me for me, and not for other reasons.

I struggle with the concept of building a community of connections. How do I be authentic if I am pursuing relationships to improve some aspect of my life? That seems self-serving. Perhaps a better approach is to seek a community that can benefit from the talents God has given each one of us. This places the focus on who you are in the community rather than what the community can offer you.

In scriptures, the Bible teaches that God knew us before we were born. God purposely gives each person talents and gifts to be used according to His will. What are your gifts? My desire to help is a gift from God. I used it to benefit my mother, and as an adult, I continue to use it to benefit others in my life.

Why is belonging to a group or being a member of a community so important? God designed us to desire a sense of belonging. We all want to be a part of something bigger than ourselves. I know I do. But to truly belong means you must share all of you with others. This means you must be you and not the person you think others want you to be – not just the part of you that you believe is acceptable – the whole you.

Brené Brown believes that we can only experience belonging at the level that we accept ourselves. If that is true, I've spent most of my life as an outcast. I have never felt worthy, and that is mainly due to the shame I felt associated with the secrecy surrounding my mother's illness. It's amazing how much one emotion can influence your behavior if you allow it.

I never understood why I always felt so ashamed and guilty. I'm a really nice person, and I generally follow the rules. But I'm also a person that hid away parts of my youth for years. Shame grows out of secrecy. The more people tried to get close to me, the more opportunity for my secret to be revealed. This secrecy empowered my sense of shame.

I hid parts of my youth to protect myself and my family from experiencing the negative impact of the stigma associated with mental illness. If I want to be authentic and develop close relationships, I must be vulnerable and expose all of me, including my past. If I don't, the shame I feel will continue to grow, and a feeling of rejection will develop. If I am vulnerable, I may get rejected anyway. It feels like a vicious cycle.

It is a vicious cycle if you continue to focus on the need to be accepted by others. The truth is that the focus should be on healthy behaviors. The research discussed earlier shows that keeping secrets are detrimental to our physical and mental health. These secrets also produce shame, which is another form of stress. We learned earlier that high levels of stress create long term medical issues. So, it's not about whether you are accepted or not. It's about viewing your world and your community with a healthy perspective – a perspective that focuses on the gifts we each bring to the table and not the value the world tries to assign to us.

What's really hard for me is trusting that others in my defined community have the same focus. In the world today, everyone seems to be focused on self-interests. Does this person want to connect with me or expose my weaknesses so that they will look better than me or feel better about themselves? Do they care about me, or do they want to use me to accomplish their personal goals? Growing up, I constantly asked these questions.

Would people understand my mother's illness or belittle me for it? Over time, I began to apply the stigma associated with mental illness to me personally. As a child, it felt like there was a stigma associated with being Jannette – not just mental illness. And this feeling carried over into adulthood.

Breaking the stronghold of this societal stigma was my first challenge to being vulnerable. I had to understand that this perception was triggered by my fear of being rejected and not any grand scheme against me. I took (and continue to take) baby steps. I slowly started sharing more of my real self with individuals I trusted. No major catastrophes occurred, so I then began to open up to a few more people.

I discovered that as you put yourself out there, it is easy to detect those seeking to self-promote instead of belong. The conversation constantly turns to their accomplishments, their beliefs and their aspirations. For every positive experience you share, they share a similar but better experience. If you can get past your personal fears, it's quite entertaining to watch.

Here's my aha! moment I want to share. To protect myself, my normal reaction was to politely avoid the self-promoters at all costs. As you can imagine, in today's society, that's a lot of people! Instead, now I try to use my gifts to be an example to the self-promoters – not as an example of perfection, but more so, as an example of being authentic by being vulnerable and sharing my whole self. Talking about my weaknesses in addition to celebrating my strengths may encourage others to do the same. Maybe, just maybe, I can be the example others need to inspire them to be themselves. Imagine it, a world of authentic people using their gifts to help one another. That's a community I want to belong in!

Barriers

What keeps us from connecting with others? For me, it was fear of rejection. My inner critic continually questioned why I thought I could bring value to others. I felt as though others would view getting to know me as a waste of time. If a person approached me for assistance, I was all in, ready to connect and help. But if I was in a room of random people, the thought of connecting made me feel anxious.

Insecurity is a significant barrier to allowing oneself to belong. You must believe you have value before you can truly connect, and to do that, requires you to accept your weaknesses. Accepting does not mean to focus on your weaknesses, but rather to acknowledge that no one is perfect, including you. It's this state of imperfection that truly connects us to one another. You may be strong in the area that I am weak in and vice versa. Together, we can accomplish more by strengthening one another than we could apart. But the only way that will happen is if we both become vulnerable and share our real selves.

What's keeping you from belonging to a community? Brené Brown states there are three things that keep most people from connecting with others: fear, resistance to vulnerability and shame. I think it is important to note many people feel shame because they view themselves in a negative manner and not because they did anything wrong. For example, I try really hard to always do what is right (an after effect of child caregiving). So, my shame doesn't come from feeling guilty for doing "bad" things. My shame comes from never feeling worthy enough to receive approval from other people. I feel bad about myself – that is shame. If you feel this way, you will have to step out of the shame lane in order to fully connect with others.

It's important to identify what triggers shame in our lives. If you identify the trigger, you can learn how to overcome the feeling and replace it with healthier thoughts. Negative thoughts formed out of shame usually draw strength when we are hiding a part of our life, keeping quiet about an area of our life, or feel judged by others because of our life. When any of the three occur, our defense mechanisms take over. This includes withdrawing from others, avoiding situations that require us to connect with others and keeping secrets. For others, people-pleasing tendencies may surface, and they try to be all things to all people, which is a disaster in the works. Finally, some people try to make others feel bad to feel better about themselves. This really sounds like an average day in middle school, doesn't it?! Been there, done that. To overcome this barrier, we need to see shame for what it truly is – fear.

Here's my challenge for you (and myself). Instead of withdrawing, hiding and trying to be invisible in an environment that requires connection, fall face first into it. Be yourself. Be honest. Be who you want to be. Showcase your talents. Don't let your inner critic steal the opportunity to share your gifts with others and to truly connect. Without this openness, you will never truly feel like you belong. It's time to let your light shine!

Share Your Gifts

I have the gift of calming difficult situations. I used it daily as a child caregiver and just about as much as an adult in the workplace. People who can remain calm can guide others through difficult situations. Staying calm helps everyone focus on the situation, not the emotions. I have found that if I remain calm, others in the room will follow my lead. However, the opposite is also true. If I act anxiously, others in the room will follow suit. For this reason, I focus on remaining calm. I grew up in an anxious household. I know how disruptive and unsettling that type of environment makes people feel. If I can bring calm into a situation and reduce everyone's anxiety, we all are in a better place to make healthy decisions that will benefit each other.

As a child, I never questioned why my mother couldn't get better. I accepted her condition without question. In fact, the thought of her being cured never crossed my mind. In my mind, the mental illness my mother struggled with was God's will. Much like Paul had a "thorn" in his side that God did not cure, my mother's thorn was anxiety. So, it made sense to believe if this is God's will, it also meant it was also God's will to create me for the sole purpose of caring for my mother. There's just one problem with this analysis. God gifted us with free will, which means we have a choice.

My mother had the choice to seek treatment and overcome her anxiety – or at least be able to manage it at a level that enabled her to stay by herself. She chose not to. Scripture also tells us that God knows everything that was, is and will be. I no longer believe I was created to care for my mother. God knew my mother would not face her mental illness, so He gave me the traits needed to survive. It was not His will for me to live only for my mother's benefit. It was his desire for me to use the gifts He gave me to benefit not only my mother but also others.

I have a friend that has the gift of hospitality. He makes people feel welcome instantly. If he is at a social event, he circles the room making everyone feel connected. Social interaction energizes him. Unfortunately, when the environment turns difficult, he uses the connections to support his personal agenda. Others watching began to question whether the interactions were sincere or not. He has a wonderful gift, but the motives behind his actions are, at times, self-serving. When self-promotion or preservation replaces authentic connections within a community, it can become a community of familiarity instead of belonging.

Everyone has a need for some level of belonging. For some people, this desire is tied to their self-worth. To belong and be accepted, these individuals may strive to fit in more than to be themselves. I hid parts of myself to "fit in." Others change parts of their self, temporarily, to fit in, especially if the person they seek acceptance from has authority. This is a slippery slope. It's okay to want to do things to please others, but there is a balance that needs to be maintained. Otherwise, you may forget which version you presented at which time and come across as a fraud.

As we discussed earlier, people-pleasing to be accepted is not healthy, and it is not needed to belong in a healthy community environment.

You have gifts as well. It's important to identify what your gifts are and share them with others. Not sure what gifts you have to offer? Think about areas that you receive the most compliments from others. What are you passionate about? What do you enjoy doing? Finally, ask God what gifts He has given you. I did. That same week three people from different areas of my life told me they valued my "wise counsel." Being able to listen to a person's concern and offer guidance is a gift from God. I didn't realize I possessed that gift until God showed me. If you ask God, he will show you the gifts He has given you.

Romans 12:6-8 states:

> Since we have gifts that differ according to the grace given to us, each of us is to use them accordingly: if prophecy, in proportion to the faith possessed; if service, in the act of serving; or he who teaches, in the act of teaching; or he who encourages, in the act of encouragement; he who gives, in the act of generosity; he who leads, with diligence; he who shows mercy, with cheerfulness.

God intended for us to use the gifts he placed inside of us to help others. We are all one piece of the community established by God. Together, we are capable of amazing things. That is why community is so important. If we are to emulate Jesus, we must make ourselves available to others. Jesus did not hide behind insecurities, he trusted God to help him accomplish his plans. He did not try to be all things to all people. He used his God-given talents to help those in need.

At one of my employers, I held a director level position. My department's team members use to say, "What would Jannette do?" when faced with a challenge. We all laughed when someone posed the question, but it gave us a starting point to try to solve the issue. I used my God-given gifts (peacemaker, encourager, wise counsel) to serve others that had different gifts. Together, we always found a solution, but it required everyone's talents; it required everyone to be present.

Have you ever been in a situation where you knew you could help, but you didn't? How did that make you feel? I'm sure it fed your inner critic nicely. Sharing your gifts and exercising the talents you have actually reduces stress. The connection you feel empowers you to do more. Don't allow fear and shame to prevent you from being all you are meant to be.

Don't ask *who* your community needs you to be. Identify who you are, what gifts you have, and *offer* those to the community. We are all needed. Don't conform to your community (people-pleasing), but instead, aspire to renew your community by offering your talents (gifts)!

How to Connect

This may be related to my past perfectionist tendencies, but I love lists! Below is a list of steps to take to establish a community of connections in your life. Remember, you are worthy, and you owe it to others to share the God-given gifts you possess.

1. Connection begins by connecting with yourself. Make a plan to take care of yourself. This includes activities that will support your physical, mental and spiritual health. To be able to help others you must first help yourself. God wants us to take care of what he has blessed us with, including our body, mind and spirit. Taking care of yourself is not selfish. It's the kindest thing you can do for your loved ones. Staying healthy will provide the strength you need to share your God-given talent with others.

2. Identify your gifts and become aware of opportunities to use them.

   In the "Share Your Gifts" section above, we discussed how to identify your gifts and the value of sharing them with others. Write down what your gifts are and keep it with you. Every day, in every circumstance, look for ways to share your gifts with others. This will not only help you connect to others, but it will increase your joy as well.

3. Accept yourself as you are – you are enough.

   I am worthy. I am enough. I am worthy. This should be your mantra. The more you say it, the more likely you will believe it. There is power in speaking words, so shout these at the top of your lungs! For additional guidance in this area, refer to the "Vulnerability" section in the "You Are Enough" chapter.

4. Do something fun.

   Being creative or playful helps rejuvenate our spirit. It reconnects us to joy. I spent so much time trying to accomplish goals that I forgot to find time to play. Do you feel physically and mentally drained most days? Do you have a to-do list that is never-ending? If you allow yourself to get burnt out at work or even at home, there will be nothing left to connect with others or to experience joy in your life. In Stuart Brown, M.D.'s book, *Play*, he discusses the necessity of play for adults and children alike. He states, "...the most significant aspect of play is that it allows us to express our joy and connect most deeply with the best in ourselves, and in others...Play is the purest expression of love."

5. Be thankful and express it regularly.

   Be thankful for everything and everyone in your life. Continuously express your thanks to God, to others and to yourself. Are you a glass half full kind of person? Make a list of things to be thankful for, and add items to it daily. Better yet, share this list with others in your life. Grumbling allows negative emotions to thrive, shifting the focus from joy to worry. So, when you feel the desire to complain about a situation, stop yourself and instead find the things that you are thankful for in the situation. For example, everyone at your workplace may appear to have gone completely mad but at least you have a paying job. You may have gained ten pounds in the last week, but thankfully, your clothes still fit. Okay, I know the challenges faced by most are more difficult than these, but the concept is the same. Replace complaints with thanks to protect your joyful attitude. If you allow negative emotions to take over your day, anxiety and worry will quickly overtake the peace and joy you have worked so hard to obtain.

6. Be passionate!

    What makes you happy? If you peel away and forget what the world tells you to do to be happy, what's left? For me, it's helping others. It can be as simple as smiling at someone in the store or holding the door open for the person behind me. The world paints a picture that helping others has to be a major production to be worthwhile. Not for me. Simple gestures that brighten another person's day brings joy to me. That is my passion.

7. Be present.

    Making yourself available to others is key if you want to belong. This is more than just attending events or gatherings. It's about being your authentic self every moment of every day. It means constantly looking for ways to share your gifts.

As I was working on this chapter of the book, I suddenly experienced a writer's block. Did I find a way to use my gifts to push through? No, I escaped by watching a movie. When I started the second two-hour movie, I realized I had a problem! The movie was my way of escaping the present because I couldn't find the words to write, which made me feel like a failure. I'm not perfect at writing. So what? If you are reading this book right now, I obviously worked through my writer's block, and I didn't do it by escaping to a movie marathon. I did by continuing to try and being present in the moment. It sounds simple, but for many of us, this is the most difficult part of connecting with others. I'll say it again – be present.

8. Wake up the next morning and do steps 1-7 again. Repeat daily.

I decided to put these steps into action one day to determine if the effort was worth the results produced. I had two medical tests scheduled at a hospital to help manage an ongoing health issue I was experiencing. The tests were minor, but it was my first time to have these particular tests, so I was anxious about the process. I decided to have a spirit of joy and trust that God would guide me through the tests successfully. And, as we discussed, joy is amplified by creating a sense of belonging. Instead of grumbling about having to take the tests, I used the opportunity to connect with the hospital staff and other patients I encountered that day.

Normally when I sit in waiting areas I look around and compare myself to everyone else. She is thinner, she is younger, he looks more professional, etc. I would convince myself I wasn't worthy of interaction and sit quietly in the corner waiting my turn. This time, I smiled at everyone that came into the area. I focused on making eye contact instead of analyzing their apparel. I was present.

When I interacted with the hospital staff I focused on the person, not just getting through the process. The in-take nurse shared with me struggles she was experiencing while caring for her elderly parents. Normally, I would have responded with a "Yes, that is difficult." Instead, I shared a similar struggle I had experienced with my mom. Our exchange provided us both the encouragement needed to handle the challenges we faced in this area. At the end of our meeting, the nurse told me it was a real pleasure to meet me. We both had smiles on our faces.

My next stop introduced me to the technician performing the tests. Instead of politely adhering to his directions, I asked him questions about his job and offered information about mine. Before I knew it, the thirty-minute test was completed, and I was off to my next stop. He seemed a little shocked when I thanked him for performing the test, but he left with a smile.

When I left the hospital at the conclusion of my tests, I had more joy than when I entered. It wasn't because the tests were done, but it was because I felt a connection with the people I encountered at the facility that day. They helped me through the tests, peacefully, by using their gifts, and I shared my thankfulness with them. Maybe this connecting thing has merit after all!

Belonging is not about being a part of a defined group. It's about connecting with others throughout your day. Community includes everyone around us. We are God's community of people. You already belong and are accepted by God. Now, use your talents to connect and help others to feel the belonging we all need in our lives. We are part of a bigger picture, God's community. Stop hiding and accept your place. More importantly, enjoy each day that has been given to you by loving others and loving yourself.

FINAL THOUGHTS

"I can do all things [which He has called me to do] through Him who strengthens and empowers me [to fulfill His purpose – I am self-sufficient in Christ's sufficiency; I am ready for anything and equal to anything through Him who infuses me with inner strength and confident peace]."
– Philippians 4:13

I wish I could tell you that once you work through the unhealthy behaviors learned in childhood, you will never have to face similar situations again. Unfortunately, that is not the case. The difference is now whenever challenges arise, you are equipped with tools that will enable you to navigate your way to healthy behaviors. Your childhood does not define you. Past actions, whether yours or someone else's, do not define you. You are a gift from God. Let your light shine!

Unless we shed light on the lasting effects of anxiety on families, it will never improve. The stigma of mental illness needs to be removed and replaced with compassion and understanding. That will not happen unless we start talking about our personal experiences. I hope this book starts the conversation for others.

Listed in the Resources section are the books, articles, and studies I read in my pursuit of discovery. If you review the list, you'll see there is truly no rhyme or reason to my sources. Each offered information that helped me understand my situation better and provide hope for the future. I encourage you to read any or all of the resources listed, but also to create your own resource list. Continue to seek your own truth, your own story.

One of the many things I learned during my journey, is that the books and research will not help you unless you first view your past with a clear lens. Remove the guilt, remove the rationalizations, and allow yourself to feel the emotions that have been bottled up inside of you. It hurts, but you will be stronger in the end.

Don't expect to read the material and instantly see results. If you take the time to absorb what you find, the lessons learned from your research will surface when needed. The key is to make sure your defense mechanisms don't kick in. I had one of those moments as I was writing this book. It seemed like every time I wrote a page a new anxiety or negative thought surfaced that I had to work through. I was so tired and thought, "Will this ever end?" At one point, I walked away from the book and didn't write anything for months.

That's when a tiny voice inside reminded me that I was not headed to a specific destination. The actual journey was what would strengthen me and enable me to find the peace and joy I desperately craved. I'm still working through my journey, but every day I am stronger, I am happier, and I am at peace. I am becoming the person God intended me to be. You can do it too. Everything you need is already inside you. You just need to peel away the layers of your past and accept the good with the bad. Then, move forward with redefining who you are and recognizing the gifts you have been given. Replace the anxiety that was woven inside you with joy, faith, hope, and love. It is possible! Don't get discouraged; you have the rest of your life to continue to battle the negative impacts of your youth.

Don't forget that we learn from each other's experiences – so share your story! God cannot use a vessel that is isolated from the world or restricted by self-doubt. Step out, shine your light and allow God to use your gifts to help others.

And do not be conformed to this world but be transformed and progressively changed by the renewing of your mind, so that you may prove what the will of God is, that which is good and acceptable and perfect. -Romans 12:2

Aspire - **R**enew - **T**ransform = The **ART** of being you!

ABOUT THE AUTHOR

Jannette McCormick is a typical, over-achieving former child caregiver searching for others. In her book "Art of Being You," Jannette encourages child caregivers to break free from the anxiety surrounding their childhood and discover God's true purpose for their lives. Jannette lives in Oklahoma with her husband Gary, and two sons Joshua and Jacob. The family also includes their Golden Retriever, Bolt, and their 100-pound Bernese Mountain lap dog, CoCo.

RESOURCES

Aldridge, J. and Becker, S. (2003). Children caring for parents with mental illness: Perspectives of young carers, parents and professionals. Bristol: Policy Press.

Anxiety and Depression Association of America. (2022). https://www.adaa.org/.

Brown, B. (2012). Daring greatly: How the courage to be vulnerable transforms the way we live, love, parent, and lead. New York: Avery.

Brown, B. (2010). The gifts of imperfection. New York: Random House.

Harris, N.B. (2018). The deepest well: Healing the long-term effects of childhood adversity. Boston: Mariner Books.

Kendall, R.T. (2012). Totally forgiving God. Florida: Charisma House.

Meyer, J. (2021). Authentically, uniquely you. New York: FaithWords.

McCormack, L., White, S., and Cuenca, J. (2016). Community work and family. 20(3):1-19.

Reinert, M., Nguyen, T., and Fritze, D. (2019). The state of mental health in America 2020. www.mhanational.org.

www.ingramcontent.com/pod-product-compliance
Lightning Source LLC
LaVergne TN
LVHW061035070526
838201LV00073B/5043